بسم الله الرحمن الرحيم

"The house of al-Arqam is the house of Islām"

Al-Ḥākim (d.405 h) in *al-Mustadrak ʿala al-Ṣaḥiḥayn* (6185)

The Virtues of Sending *Ṣalāt* on the Prophet

صلى الله عليه وعلى آله وسلم

فضل الصلاة على النبي

صلى الله عليه وآله وسلم

Al-Imām Ismāʿīl b. Isḥāq al-Qāḍī

(d. 282/895)

Translated by Amr Abu Ayyub

DAR AL-ARQAM

ISBN: 978-0-9928136-9-7

British Library Cataloguing in Publishing Data
A catalogue record for this book is available from the British Library

Prepared and published by Dar al-Arqam Publishing,
Birmingham, United Kingdom

Translated by Amr Abu Ayyub

He is a student of Islamic knowledge based in the United States. He has a number of *ijāzāt* in ḥadīth and Qurʾān, and has been engaged in the study of Islamic law for a decade. His interests include Islamic legal theory, objectives of the Sharīʿah, development of Islamic legal systems, exegesis of the Qurʾān, and theology.

Edited by Adnan Karim

Head of translation at Dar al-Arqam. He has translated and edited a number of works for Dar al-Arqam.

www.daral-arqam.co.uk
Email: daralarqam@hotmail.co.uk

Printed by Mega Printing in Turkey

THE VIRTUES OF SENDING

ṢALĀT ON THE PROPHET

صَلَّى ٱللَّهُ عَلَيْهِ وَسَلَّمَ

Al-Imām Ismāʿīl b. Isḥāq al-Qāḍī
(d. 282/895)

DAR AL-ARQAM

الفهرس
Contents

مقدمة المترجم
Translator's Introduction

All praise belongs to Allāh, Lord of the Worlds, and may His *ṣalāt* and *salām* be upon His slave and messenger, Muḥammad, and upon his family and supporters.

Allāh ﷻ said:

إِنَّ اللَّهَ وَمَلَائِكَتَهُ يُصَلُّونَ عَلَى النَّبِيِّ يَا أَيُّهَا الَّذِينَ آمَنُوا صَلُّوا عَلَيْهِ وَسَلِّمُوا تَسْلِيمًا ﴿٥٦﴾

> {Indeed, Allāh and His angels send *ṣalāt* upon the Prophet. Believers! Invoke *ṣalāt* upon him, and salute him with worthy greetings of peace.} [Qur'ān 33:56]

عن عبد الله بن مسعود رضي الله تعالىٰ عنه، أنَّ رسول الله ﷺ قال: «أولىٰ النَّاس بي يوم القيامة أكثرُهم عليَّ صلاةً» [الترمذيُّ: ٤٨٤]

ʿAbdullāh b. Masʿud رضي الله عنه reported that Allāh's Messenger ﷺ said, **"The worthiest people of me on the Day of Resurrection are those who offers the most *ṣalāt* on me."** (Reported by al-Tirmidhī, 484)

عن أبي بن كعب رضي الله تعالىٰ عنه أنه قال لرسول الله ﷺ: يا رسولَ اللهِ

إِنِّي أُكْثِرُ الصلاةَ عليْكَ فكم أجعَلُ لكَ من صلاتِي فقال «ما شِئْتَ» قال: قلتُ: الربعَ، قال: «ما شئْتَ فإِنْ زدتَّ فهو خيرٌ لكَ»، قلتُ: النصفَ، قال: «ما شئتَ فإِنْ زدتَّ فهو خيرٌ لكَ»، قال: قلْتُ: فالثلثينِ، قال: «ما شئْتَ فإِنْ زدتَّ فهو خيرٌ لكَ» قلتُ: أجعلُ لكَ صلاتي كلَّها، قال: «إذًا تُكفَىٰ همَّكَ ويغفرْ لكَ ذنبُكَ».

Ubayy b. Kaʿb ﷺ reported that he said to the Messenger of Allāh ﷺ: "Messenger of Allāh, I offer many *ṣalāt* on you. How much of my supplications should be dedicated to you?" He replied, **"However much you wish."** Ubayy said, "A fourth?" He replied, **"Whatever you wish, but if you did more, it is good."** Ubayy said, "A half?" The Prophet ﷺ replied, **"Whatever you wish, but if you did more, it is good."** Ubayy said, "Two thirds?" The Prophet ﷺ replied, **"Whatever you wish, but if you did more, it is good."** Ubayy said, "How about all of it?" The Prophet ﷺ replied, **"If you did so, your worries will be sufficed, and your sins will be forgiven."**[1] (Reported by al-Tirmidhī, 2457)

In commenting on this narration, al-Imām al-Ṭībī said, "The man said, 'I will make all of my prayers for you,' which means 'instead of supplicating for myself, I will just send *ṣalāt* upon you,' and the response was, **'If you did so, your worries will be sufficed, and your sins will be forgiven.'** Meaning, all that you worry about in your religion and worldly matters [will be sufficed]. The reason is that *ṣalāt* upon the Prophet ﷺ consists of remembrance of Allāh and honouring of the Messenger ﷺ. One busies themselves with

1 Reported by al-Tirmidhī (2457) and it is an authentic ḥadīth, as stated by al-Tirmidhī.

fulfilling [the Messenger's] rights over their own goals, and when one prefers him in supplication over their own selves, what honourable qualities they are! And what fruitful, noble actions they have done!'"[2]

Al-Imām Mullā 'Alī al-Qārī ﵀ quotes al-Abharī, "If you spent all of your time supplicating by just sending *ṣalāt* upon me, you will be sufficed of all of your worries."[3] Therefore, the reason why the scholars mention this is to show that there is a higher level of supplication and worship, above what others do. It is where one does not even busy themselves with their own supplications or selves, but only supplicate via *ṣalāt* upon Allāh's Messenger ﷺ.

Undoubtedly, *ṣalāt* upon the Messenger of Allāh ﷺ is of the highest actions of worship that one can do. How can one resist uttering *ṣalāt* upon the Prophet ﷺ; he who gave his life, his money, his time, his efforts, his children, his companions and friends, his rest, his worldly life, and sacrificed it all, just to teach you, dear Muslim, about monotheism and to warn you from polytheism? Indeed, the greatest of the creation of Allāh is Muḥammad. He is the noblest of men, the finest of humans, the greatest of worshippers, the bravest of warriors, the humblest of servants. He was the light that beckoned, the chief of creation, the *khalīl* of Allāh, the carrier of His final message.

Muḥammad ﷺ holds a special place in the hearts of all who know him, and those who do not hold him in high regard simply do not know him. How can one learn of and know this most honourable of men, yet still deny or belie him? How can one learn of his sacrifices and still resist the urge to say with full conviction and with the utmost love, *ṣalla 'llāhu 'alayhi wa sallam*.

---

2 *Sharḥ al-Mishkāt* by al-Ṭībī (3/1046).
3 *Mirqāt al-Mafātīḥ Sharḥ Mishkāt al-Maṣābīḥ* (2/746).

In my translation, I have opted to not translate the word *ṣalāt* into any particular word, instead leaving it transliterated. The reason is that there is so much knowledge contained in just this word, that leaving it transliterated is far more serving to our needs and goals.

Surely, the *ṣalāt* on the Prophet ﷺ has a meaning. Unfortunately, few understand it, and yet instead of learning its meaning and implementing it in their lives, they would instead choose to dissuade Muslims from uttering the *ṣalāt* upon the Messenger of Allāh ﷺ. With that said, there is a difference of opinion on what it means as it pertains to Allāh, the angels, and humankind.

One view cited by the scholars is what al-Imām Ibn Kathīr said, "Al-Bukhārī ؒ said that Abu 'l-'Āliyah ؒ said, 'When Allāh sends *ṣalāt*, it refers to His praise [of the person] in the presence of the angels. When the angels offer *ṣalāt* [on a person], it refers to their supplications [for them].' Ibn 'Abbas ؓ also said, 'They send *ṣalāt*, meaning, they ask Allāh for blessings [for the person].'"[4] Ibn Kathīr would then mention, "It was reported from Sufyān al-Thawrī and many other scholars that the *ṣalāt* of the Lord is mercy, and the *ṣalāt* of the angels is seeking forgiveness."[5]

Another view that is cited is that of al-Imām al-Ṭabarī in commentary of the verse:

أُولَٰئِكَ عَلَيْهِمْ صَلَوَاتٌ مِّن رَّبِّهِمْ وَرَحْمَةٌ ۖ وَأُولَٰئِكَ هُمُ الْمُهْتَدُونَ ﴿١٥٧﴾

{Those are the ones upon whom there is *ṣalāt* from their Lord, and mercy as well; and those are the ones who are on

4 *Tafsīr Ibn Kathīr* (6/457).
5 Ibid.

the right path} [Qur'ān 2:157]

In commenting on this verse, al-Ṭabarī said, "Allāh ﷻ means to say, 'Those patient ones whom I have described and characterised, they have *ṣalāt*, i.e. pardoning. The *ṣalāt* of Allāh upon His slaves means His pardoning of His slaves. This is similar to what was narrated from the Prophet ﷺ, **'Allāh, send *ṣalāt* upon the family of Abū Awfā.'** Meaning, forgive them. When He said, ***'And mercy,'*** it means, along with the pardoning with which He forgave and concealed their sins, they will have mercy and compassion from Allāh."

Al-Imām Ibn 'Āshūr said, "The reality of *ṣalāt* in the language of the Arabs is that it refers to statements that indicate love of goodness for a person. For that reason, the most popular of its definitions is simply, 'supplication.' For this reason, as well, attributing the action to the One from whom all goodness is sought is metaphorically necessary to establish the meaning, which is the advent of goodness. As such, when *ṣalāt* is ascribed to Allāh, it indicates Mercy and conveyance of benefit, such as His Mercy, forgiveness, or purification."[6]

In addition to these views, al-Ṭabarī cites other views on the topic, stating, for example, that *ṣalāt* means, "They invoke blessings upon the Prophet Muḥammad ﷺ." He cites this view from Ibn 'Abbās, who said, "It means that they invoke blessings upon the Prophet." Ibn al-Jawzī cites five views in his book, *Zād al-Masīr*:

1. That it is the Mercy of Allāh. This was the view of al-Ḥasan al-Baṣrī.
2. That it is the forgiveness of Allāh. This was the view of Sa'īd b.

6 *Tafsīr al-Taḥrīr wa 'l-Tanwīr* (2/57-58).

Jubayr.

3. That it is the praise of Allāh. This was the view of Abu 'l-'Āliyah.
4. That it is His honouring of the person. This was the view of Sufyān.
5. That it is the blessings of Allāh. This was the view of Abū 'Ubaydah.

Further, when citing the views on what the *ṣalāt* of the angels means, he states there are two varying views:

1. That it means they supplicate for him. This was the view of Abu 'l-'Āliyah.
2. That it means they ask Allāh to forgive the person. This was the view of Muqātil.[7]

Note, dear reader, that in this instance, we can state that these views are not mutually exclusive. When there are conflicting views and they are mutually inclusive, it means we can accept all of these interpretations. As such, the *ṣalāt* of Allāh and His angels, respectively, mean all of these things. Think: If *ṣalāt* meant mercy, does that conflict with forgiveness? Does it conflict with praise from Allāh, or His honouring of the person, or the blessings He bestows? They are mutually inclusive. As such, this further shows why I chose to omit any translation of the actual word, *ṣalāt*, and instead opted to keep the word as is, for one English word will restrict the vastness of this word in the works of the exegetes.

7 *Zād al-Masīr* (3/470).

Al-Imām al-Zamakhsharī states, "The praying person bends in their bowing and prostration, and as such, the word *ṣalāt* was metaphorically used to refer to someone who curves or bends towards a person out of compassion, resembling a person visiting the sick out of their compassion, and a woman in her compassion towards her child. The meaning was used so frequently in this manner until it was used to refer to mercy and compassion." The reason why this quote is so important is that some may claim that al-Imām al-Zamakhsharī ﷺ opted for the view that *ṣalāt* does not actually refer to saying *ṣalla 'llāhu 'alayhi wa sallam*, but a mere feeling of compassion that occurs within oneself. How can this be the case when he states, "If 'May Allāh send *ṣalāt* upon you,' means, 'May Allāh show mercy and compassion to you,' then what of the verse **{It is He who sends *ṣalāt* upon you, as well as His angels}**? What does the *ṣalāt* of the angels refer to? My view is that it refers to them saying, 'Allāh, send *ṣalāt* upon the believers.'"[8] As can be clearly seen, al-Zamakhsharī believes it refers to actions of the tongue.

When Allāh ﷻ said:

إِنَّ اللَّهَ وَمَلَائِكَتَهُ يُصَلُّونَ عَلَى النَّبِيِّ يَا أَيُّهَا الَّذِينَ آمَنُوا صَلُّوا عَلَيْهِ وَسَلِّمُوا
تَسْلِيمًا ﴿٥٦﴾

> {Indeed, Allāh and His angels send *ṣalāt* upon the Prophet. Believers! Invoke *ṣalāt* upon him, and salute him with worthy greetings of peace.} [Qur'ān 33:56]

Did the scholars infer that it is recommended or obligatory to utter *ṣalāt* upon the Prophet ﷺ? The answer is quite clearly, yes. I will

---

8 *Tafsīr al-Kashshāf* (3/545).

suffice with a few examples from the books of the Muslim jurists. For example, al-Shaykh Manṣūr b. Yūnus al-Buhūtī says in his book, *al-Rawḍ al-Murbiʿ* (an elementary work in Ḥanbalī law), "*Ṣalāt* upon the Prophet ﷺ is recommended, and that recommendation becomes emphasised on the day and night of Friday. Likewise, [it is recommended] every time his name is mentioned. Some stated that it is obligatory." It is quite clear that the scholars understood that one should utter the *ṣalāt* therefore, and that this verse does not just mean a feeling in the heart. Apart from that fact, when this verse was revealed, as we will come to learn in this very book, the companions approached the Prophet ﷺ and said, "Messenger of Allāh, we know how to salute you, but how is the *ṣalāt* done?" The Prophet ﷺ would respond by telling them of *al-ṣalāt al-ibrāhīmiyyah*, and informed them how to send *ṣalāt* upon him.

It is also unfortunate that some Muslims take the concept of *ṣalāt* as meaning a feeling of support or having empathy towards the Messenger ﷺ. Such a faulty explanation is so faulty that simply mentioning it serves as sufficient reason to boycott it. Indeed, the many aḥādīth mentioned in this short book show that it encompasses much more than just having a feeling of support, but rather, it means to sit down and reflect on these statements of the Messenger ﷺ and even state out loud, *ṣalla 'llāhu 'alā Muḥammad*, just as he taught his noble companions. Yes, this *ṣalāt* is not an empty ritual, but an act of devotion to Allāh and to His Messenger. It is an act of appreciation of Muḥammad; indeed, the highest in rank, the angels, send *ṣalāt* upon Muḥammad, yet we, the fallible, feeble, and weak humans who rely on his perfect conveyance of the message, find in ourselves all reasons to withhold this most basic portrayal of love and conviction. Woe unto us.

Apart from this fact, the Muslim should be aware that when Allāh's Messenger ﷺ told the believers how to send *ṣalāt* upon him, he also included his family, as can be seen in this book. But that begs the question: Who are the family *(āl)* of the Prophet ﷺ? The scholars have differed on the *Āl* of the Messenger. To summarise the views of the scholars on this topic, it includes the wives of the Prophet ﷺ, the Tribe of Hāshim, the Tribe of al-Muṭṭalib, and the respective freed slaves of those two tribes.

The wives of the prophets are considered a part of their family, and that applies to all prophets, let alone our Messenger ﷺ. The evidence is that, when referring to Ibrāhīm عليه السلام, Allāh said:

قَالُوٓا أَتَعْجَبِينَ مِنْ أَمْرِ ٱللَّهِ ۖ رَحْمَتُ ٱللَّهِ وَبَرَكَٰتُهُۥ عَلَيْكُمْ أَهْلَ ٱلْبَيْتِ ۚ إِنَّهُۥ حَمِيدٌ مَّجِيدٌ ﴿٧٣﴾

> {They said, "Do you marvel at Allāh's command? Allāh's mercy and His blessings have always been upon you, O people of the house. Surely, He is Praiseworthy, Glorious."} [Qur'ān 11:73]

When commenting on this verse, al-Qurṭubī said, "This verse proves that a man's wife is considered a part of his '*ahl al-bayt* (household).' This shows that the wives of all prophets are from their households. As such, 'Ā'ishah رضي الله عنها is a part of the *Ahl al-Bayt* of the Prophet ﷺ." Therefore, the wives of Muḥammad are considered a part of his household. Apart from that, the Messenger ﷺ said – as reported in this book, in narration number 70 – that when teaching how to send *ṣalāt*, the Prophet ﷺ said, **"Say: Allāh, send *ṣalāt* upon Muḥammad, his wives, and his offspring, just as you have sent *ṣalāt***

upon the family of Ibrāhīm, and send blessings upon Muḥammad, his wives, and his offspring, just as you have sent blessings upon the family of Ibrāhīm. Truly, you are Praiseworthy and Glorious."[9] As such, when taking this ḥadīth into account, as well as the many aḥādīth that mention the **"family"** of the Prophet, we can conclude that this particular ḥadīth is particularising the **"family"** of the Prophet ﷺ and is including his wives.

Even more specific of an evidence is the long passage in the Qur'ān addressed to the wives of the Prophet ﷺ in Sūrat al-Aḥzāb, verses 32-34. At the end of those verses, Allāh said:

إِنَّمَا يُرِيدُ ٱللَّهُ لِيُذْهِبَ عَنكُمُ ٱلرِّجْسَ أَهْلَ ٱلْبَيْتِ وَيُطَهِّرَكُمْ تَطْهِيرًا ﴿٣٣﴾

{Allāh wishes to keep uncleanness away from you, people of the [Prophet's] House, and to purify you thoroughly.} [Qur'ān 33:33]

As such, after addressing the wives of the Prophet ﷺ in many commandments, Allāh concludes those verses by referring to them as being a part of the Family of the Prophet ﷺ. Of the scholars who held this view was 'Ikrimah ﷺ. Al-Ṭabarī reports that he would cite this verse in the marketplaces and say, "This verse was revealed specifically about the wives of the Prophet ﷺ."

With that said, the majority held that this verse was about 'Alī, Fāṭimah, al-Ḥasan, and al-Ḥusayn. This is proven by a number of aḥādīth of Allāh's Messenger ﷺ. For example, 'Ā'ishah ﷺ reports, "The Messenger ﷺ once set out during the morning, wearing a black blanket with cauldron patterns on it. Al-Ḥasan b. 'Alī then

9 Reported by al-Bukhārī (3369) and Muslim (407).

came, and he pulled him into the blanket. Then, al-Ḥusayn came and he entered with him. Then Fāṭimah came, and he pulled her under the blanket, and then 'Alī came and he pulled him into the blanket. He then recited, **{Allāh wishes to keep uncleanness away from you, people of the [Prophet's] House, and to purify you thoroughly.}**"[10] Another narration states that the Prophet ﷺ said, **"Allāh, these are the members of my household,"** when referring to them.[11]

However, these are special incidents that do not exclude others from his household, as proven by the linguistic usage of the word *āl* in the Qur'ān, and as proven by the Prophet ﷺ including all of the Tribe of Hāshim and the Tribe of al-Muṭṭalib in his household, as shall be seen.

Another verse that proves this usage of *al-āl* refers to the wives of a prophet is when Allāh said of the noble prophet, Lūṭ ﵇:

قَالُوٓاْ إِنَّآ أُرۡسِلۡنَآ إِلَىٰ قَوۡمٖ مُّجۡرِمِينَ ٥٨ إِلَّآ ءَالَ لُوطٍ إِنَّا لَمُنَجُّوهُمۡ أَجۡمَعِينَ ٥٩ إِلَّا ٱمۡرَأَتَهُۥ قَدَّرۡنَآ إِنَّهَا لَمِنَ ٱلۡغَٰبِرِينَ ٦٠

> {They (the angels) said: "We have been sent to a people who are criminals, but We shall save the household of Lot, all except his wife: We have decreed that she will be one of those who stay behind.} [Qur'ān 15:58-60]

As can be seen from these verses, Allāh declares that He shall save the family of Lūṭ, except for his wife, indicating that she is considered a

---

10 Reported by Muslim (2424).

11 Reported by al-Ḥākim (4764).

part of his *āl*.

Further, the *Āl* of Muḥammad includes the two tribes, al-Muṭṭalib and Hāshim. This was the view of al-Imām Aḥmad[12] and others, and the evidence cited is that the Prophet ﷺ said, as reported by Jubayr b. Muṭʿim, **"The Tribe of Hāshim and the Tribe of al-Muṭṭalib are one,"** and then intertwined his fingers.[13] This ḥadīth would serve to prove that both the Tribes of Hāshim and al-Muṭṭalib, the two sons of ʿAbd Manāf are considered to be part of the *Āl* of Allāh's Messenger ﷺ. As for why other sons of ʿAbd Manāf are not included, the Prophet ﷺ clarified, **"They did not abandon me during the times of ignorance nor during the times of Islām."**[14]

The families of the Tribe of Hāshim in particular that are considered a part of the *Āl* of the Prophet ﷺ are:

- The offspring of al-ʿAbbās b. ʿAbd al-Muṭṭalib.
- The offspring of ʿAlī b. Abī Ṭālib.
- The offspring of Jaʿfar b. Abī Ṭālib.
- The offspring of ʿAqīl b. Abī Ṭālib.
- The offspring of al-Ḥārith b. ʿAbd al-Muṭṭalib.
- The offspring of Abū Lahab b. ʿAbd al-Muṭṭalib.[15]

---

12 Refer to *Sharḥ Muntahā al-Irādāt* (1/642).
13 Reported by al-Bukhārī (2907).
14 Reported by al-Nasāʾī (4148) and Ibn al-Mulaqqin declared it to be authentic in *al-Badr al-Munīr* (7/317).
15 Refer to *Kashshāf al-Qināʿ* (2/290-291).

The evidence to this is the ḥadīth that al-Imām Aḥmad reported from Zayd b. Arqam, who said:

> One day Allāh's Messenger ﷺ stood up to deliver a sermon at a watering place known as Khumm, situated between Makkah and Madīnah. He praised Allāh, extolled Him and delivered the sermon and admonished us, saying, **'As to what follows: People, I am a human being. I am about to receive a messenger (the angel of death) from my Lord and I, in response to Allāh's call, shall respond in turn (meaning, pass away). I leave among you two weighty things: The first being the Book of Allāh in which there is guidance and light, so hold fast to the Book of Allāh and adhere to it.'** He then admonished us regarding the Book of Allāh, encouraging us [to hold fast to it]. He then said, **'Next is my household. I implore you to observe Allāh regarding my household. I implore you to observe Allāh regarding my household. I implore you to observe Allāh regarding my household.'"**
>
> Huṣayn said, 'Who are the members of his household? Are not his wives the members of his family?' He responded, 'His wives are the members of his family [but here] the members of his family are those for whom acceptance of *zakāt* is forbidden.' He replied, 'Who are they?' Zayd responded, 'The offspring of ʿAlī, The offspring of ʿAqīl, the offspring of Jaʿfar, and the offspring of al-ʿAbbās.'[16]

It befits the Muslim, that when offering *ṣalāt* upon the Messenger

16 Reported by Muslim (2408).

ﷺ to remember that it is the Sunnah to also send *ṣalāt* upon his *Āl*, and his *Āl* includes these people, may the peace and blessings of Allāh be upon them.

In this remarkable, yet short treatise, al-Qāḍī Ismāʿīl beautifully clarifies the virtues, meaning, wordings, and timings of saying *ṣalāt* upon the Messenger ﷺ. Al-Qāḍī Ismāʿīl al-Azdī is a great luminary of this Ummah, a giant upon whose shoulders rest many foundational sciences of Islām. He was a scholar of language, rivalling the greats of his time, al-Mubarrad and Thaʿlab, a scholar of ḥadīth, having learned its nuances and defect *(ʿilal)* detection from the master himself, ʿAlī b. al-Madīnī, a scholar of Qurʾān, comprising of all of its sciences, including its exegesis and variants of reading. His books are worthwhile, his knowledge is enduring, and his contributions are appreciated.

My work on this book was quite simple, and for that I am thankful to al-Shaykh Muḥammad al-Albānī, the Albanian and Damascene scholar of ḥadīth, for he published this book many decades ago.

1. His publication consists of one hundred and seven narrations, on which he offered his judgements as to their authenticity or lack thereof. True, there is another publication of this work by Dār al-Kutub al-ʿIlmiyyah, but it was found wanting. As such, I relied fully on the edition of al-Shaykh al-Albānī. May Allāh have mercy upon him.

2. I have supplemented some of his judgements with those mentioned by other scholars of ḥadīth, such as al-Ḥākim, Ibn Rajab, Ibn Ḥajar, or other early scholars of ḥadīth.

3. He has also referenced many of the narrations to other sources

and supplemented inauthentic chains of narration with authentic ones, though sometimes, they are not mentioned. In those cases, I have referenced them myself, and added the numbers of the narrations in their respective sources. Sometimes, I did this because the chain of narration of al-Qāḍī Ismāʿīl was inauthentic, and I sought to supplement his chain of narration with an authentic one, and sometimes, al-Shaykh al-Albānī referenced the books to their volumes and pages, whereas the common practice in contemporary times is to reference the narration number in the respective works.

4. Any notes I add will be denoted with the [T] mark, in order to delineate between mine and al-Albānī's words.

I ask Allāh to accept from us this humble effort, which is meant to encourage all Muslims to utter more *ṣalāt* upon the Messenger of Allāh ﷺ. If just one person reads this and utters *ṣalāt* upon the Prophet ﷺ then it will have served its purpose.

Lastly, may Allāh send *ṣalāt* and *salām* upon Muḥammad, and upon his wives and offspring.

Amr Abu Ayyub
24th June 2022

ترجمة المؤلف
Biography of the Author[17]

His Titles, Name, Lineage, and Birth:

He was the Imām, Shaykh al-Islām, Abū Isḥāq Ismāʿīl b. Isḥāq b. Ismāʿīl b. Ḥammād b. Zayd (the great scholar of ḥadith) al-Azdī. He would reside initially in al-Baṣrah, and then move to Baghdād. He was the author of many works, and was the greatest scholar of the Mālikī *madhhab* of his times. He was born in the year 199 *hijrī*.

His Studies

He studied with a number of great scholars of Islām and shared many teachers with al-Imām al-Bukhārī ﷺ. He was given a blessed life, such that he had an abundance of very short chains of narrations to the Prophet ﷺ. Many would learn narrations and knowledge from him that they could not learn anywhere else. When people would travel to learn from him, each person would learn unique knowledge; some people would learn things about ḥadīth, and some would learn about Qurʾān, *qirāʾāt*, law, and so forth.

Al-Imām Abū ʿAmr al-Dānī, one of the great scholars of the Qurʾān and its variant readings, once said, "He learned recitations from Qālūn and even had his own variant in recitation."[18] Al-Imām

17 Taken mainly from *Tārīkh Baghdād* of al-Khaṭīb al-Baghdādī (6/281-287) and *Siyar Aʿlām al-Nubalāʾ* by al-Ḥāfiẓ Shams al-Dīn al-Dhahabī (13/339-342).

18 *Tartīb al-Madārik wa Taqrīb al-Masālik* (4/282).

Qālūn was the student of Nāfiʿ and possesses one of the ten concurrent recitations of the Qurʾān. It is read widely in North African lands east of Morocco, such as Libya and some parts of Tunisia, may Allāh protect them both.

His Travels, Studies, Positions, and Scholarly Contributions

He lived in Baghdād and was made its judge for approximately forty years. He was a just judge. Most of his time, after settling disputes as a judge, was spent in knowledge. Initially, he was the judge of the Eastern Sector of Baghdād. Then, approximately seventeen years later, he was made the judge of the entirety of Baghdād, after the death of Siwār b. ʿAbdillāh. Due to his understanding and bravery, he was the first to allow some to testify and prevent others from testifying, depending on their uprightness. He said, "People have become corrupt."

He authored *al-Musnad* (in ḥadīth) and other books about the sciences of the Qurʾān. He gathered the narrations of Mālik, Yaḥyā b. Saʿīd al-Anṣārī, and Ayyūb al-Sakhtiyānī. He was also a scholar of the Arabic Language, for al-Mubarrad said about him, "He is more knowledgeable about morphology than I am."

He learned *fiqh* from Aḥmad b. al-Muʿaddal[19] and ḥadīth and its defects from ʿAlī b. al-Madīnī, the teacher of al-Imām al-Bukhārī, about whom al-Bukhārī said, "I never felt small in knowledge before anyone but ʿAlī b. al-Madīnī."[20]

---

19 Al-Dhahabī mentioned that he was a great Mālikī scholar, and the student of ʿAbd al-Malik b. al-Mājishūn and Muḥammad b. Maslamah.
20 *Siyar Aʿlām al-Nubalāʾ* (11/46).

He was a virtuous scholar and was proficient in the *madhhab* of al-Imām Mālik. He explained and summarised his *madhhab*. He became so proficient in *fiqh* that he became a luminary. He spread the *madhhab* of Mālik in Baghdād such that it was never spread before. He also wrote books proving the veracity of the positions held by al-Imām Mālik and explaining them, and they were used by the students of the Mālikī *madhhab* with great concern and care.

In addition to that, he was a scholar of the Qur'ān; he wrote many books about the Qur'ān, such as *Aḥkām al-Qur'ān*. He was the first to write on this topic amongst the followers of the Mālikī school. He also wrote a book about the variant readings of the Qur'ān and a book on exegesis.

Ibn al-Muntāb said, "I heard Isma'ıl, the Judge, say, 'I once visited Yaḥyā b. Aktham and in his presence were people debating on matters pertaining to law. They were saying, 'The people of Madīnah say,' and when he saw me approaching, he said, 'Madīnah has come!'" Further, al-Qāḍī Abu 'l-Walīd al-Bājī once said of him, after mentioning the scholars who have reached the level of *mujtahid* and gathered encyclopedic knowledge of all sciences, "None reached this level after Mālik except Ismā'īl al-Qāḍī."[21]

Due to his religiosity, he was respected by even the leaders. The Caliph of the time, al-Mu'taḍid, once wrote to his governor, "Treat the two virtuous *shaykhs* well: Ismā'īl b. Isḥāq and Mūsā b. Isḥāq, for they are people who, when Allāh wishes to punish residents of a land, He diverts His punishment due to their supplications." After the death of his mother, Abu 'l-'Abbās al-Mubarrad comments, "I

21 *Tartīb al-Madārik wa Taqrīb al-Masālik* (4/282).

rode to him to console him; I pained for him. I found with him the greatest members of the Tribe of Hāshim (the family of the Prophet ﷺ), the jurists, the upright, and those with good conduct in Baghdād. I saw him showing deep grief, while all were consoling him, but he almost could not console himself." Al-Mubarrad mentioned that he would then mention some poetry to him to console him, after which, al-Qāḍī Ismāʿīl recovered and some happiness showed in his face, and he wrote the lines of poetry down.[22]

His Students

Some of his students include:

- ʿAbdullāh, the son of Aḥmad b. Ḥanbal.
- Mūsā b. Hārūn.
- Abū Bakr b. al-Najjād.
- Abū Bakr al-Shāfiʿī.
- Muḥammad b. Khalaf al-Qāḍī, known better as Wakīʿ.

His Death

He died suddenly in the year 282 *hijrī*, may Allāh have mercy upon him.

22 *Tartīb al-Madārik wa Taqrīb al-Masālik* (4/283-284).

فضل الصلاة على النبي

صلى الله عليه وآله وسلم

بسم الله الرحمن الرحيم

In the Name of Allāh, Most Merciful, the Giver of Mercy

١ - أَنْبَأَنَا إِسْمَاعِيلُ بْنُ أَبِي أُوَيْسٍ، حَدَّثَنِي أَخِي، عَنْ سُلَيْمَانَ بْنِ بِلَالٍ، عَنْ عُبَيْدِ اللهِ بْنِ عُمَرَ، عَنْ ثَابِتٍ الْبُنَانِيِّ، قَالَ أَنَسُ بْنُ مَالِكٍ: قَالَ أَبُو طَلْحَةَ: إِنَّ رَسُولَ اللهِ ﷺ خَرَجَ عَلَيْهِمْ يَوْمًا يَعْرِفُونَ الْبِشْرَ فِي وَجْهِهِ فَقَالُوا إِنَّا نَعْرِفُ الْآنَ فِي وَجْهِكَ الْبِشْرَ يَا رَسُولَ اللهِ، قَالَ: «**أَجَلْ، أَتَانِي الْآنَ آتٍ مِنْ رَبِّي فَأَخْبَرَنِي أَنَّهُ لَنْ يُصَلِّيَ عَلَيَّ أَحَدٌ مِنْ أُمَّتِي إِلَّا رَدَّهَا اللهُ عَلَيْهِ عَشْرَ أَمْثَالِهَا**».

1. Anas b. Mālik said that Abū Ṭalḥah ﵁ reported that Allāh's Messenger ﷺ once approached them, such that they recognised the glee in his face. They said to him, "We recognise the glee in your face, Messenger of Allāh!" He responded, **"Indeed; a messenger came to me now from my Lord and informed me that not a single member of my Ummah sends *ṣalāt* upon me but that Allāh reciprocates it for them ten-fold."**[23]

٢ - حَدَّثَنَا سُلَيْمَانُ بْنُ حَرْبٍ، قَالَ أَنْبَأَنَا حَمَّادُ بْنُ سَلَمَةَ، عَنْ ثَابِتٍ الْبُنَانِيِّ، عَنْ سُلَيْمَانَ، مَوْلَى الْحَسَنِ بْنِ عَلِيٍّ، عَنْ عَبْدِ اللهِ بْنِ أَبِي طَلْحَةَ،

---

23 Reported by al-Bayhaqī (1561) and Aḥmad (16399) and al-Albānī said it is authentic.

عَنْ أَبِيهِ، أَنَّ رَسُولَ اللهِ ﷺ جَاءَ يَوْمًا وَالْبِشْرُ يُرَىٰ فِي وَجْهِهِ فَقَالُوا: يَا رَسُولَ اللهِ إِنَّا نَرَىٰ فِي وَجْهِكَ بِشْرًا لَمْ نَكُنْ نَرَاهُ قَالَ: «**أَجَلْ إِنَّهُ أَتَانِي مَلَكٌ، فَقَالَ: يَا مُحَمَّدُ إِنَّ رَبَّكَ يَقُولُ: أَمَا يُرْضِيكَ أَلَّا يُصَلِّيَ عَلَيْكَ أَحَدٌ مِنْ أُمَّتِكَ إِلَّا صَلَّيْتُ عَلَيْهِ عَشْرًا وَلَا سَلَّمَ عَلَيْكَ إِلَّا سَلَّمْتُ عَلَيْهِ عَشْرًا؟**»

2. Abū Ṭalḥah said: "Allāh's Messenger ﷺ once approached, and glee could be seen glaringly in his face. They said to him, 'Messenger of Allāh, we see glee in your face that we have never seen before.' He replied, **"Indeed; an angel came to me and said, 'Muḥammad, your Lord says: "Does it not please you that there is not a member of your Ummah who sends *ṣalāt* upon you, but that I send ten *ṣalāt* upon them, nor sends their salutations upon you, but that I send ten salutations to them?"'"**"[24]

٣ - حَدَّثَنَا إِسْحَاقُ بْنُ مُحَمَّدٍ الْفَرْوِيُّ، قَالَ ثنا أَبُو طَلْحَةَ الْأَنْصَارِيُّ، عَنْ أَبِيهِ، عَنْ إِسْحَاقَ بْنِ عَبْدِ اللهِ بْنِ أَبِي طَلْحَةَ، عَنْ أَبِيهِ، عَنْ جَدِّهِ، قَالَ: قَالَ رَسُولُ اللهِ ﷺ: «**مَنْ صَلَّىٰ عَلَيَّ وَاحِدَةً صَلَّىٰ اللهُ عَلَيْهِ عَشْرًا فَلْيُكْثِرْ عَبْدٌ مِنْ ذَلِكَ أَوْ لِيُقِلَّ**».

3. Abū Ṭalḥah ﷺ said that Allāh's Messenger ﷺ said: **"Whoever sends one *ṣalāt* upon me, Allāh sends ten *ṣalāt* upon them.**

24 Reported by Aḥmad (16361) and al-Nasā'ī (1295). Al-Ḥāfiẓ Mughulṭāy said its chain of narration is authentic in *Sharḥ Ibn Mājah* (3/517) and al-Ḥāfiẓ al-'Irāqī said its chain of narration is great in *Takhrīj Iḥyā' 'Ulūm al-Dīn* (1/408).

Therefore, let [a slave]²⁵ do so often, or infrequently."²⁶

٤ – حَدَّثَنَا عَبْدُ اللهِ بْنُ مَسْلَمَةَ قَالَ: ثنا سَلَمَةُ بْنُ وَرْدَانَ، قَالَ: سَمِعْتُ
أَنَسَ بْنَ مَالِكٍ، قَالَ: خَرَجَ النَّبِيُّ ﷺ يَتَبَرَّزُ، فَلَمْ يَجِدْ أَحَدًا يَتْبَعُهُ، فَهَرَعَ
عُمَرُ فَاتَّبَعَهُ بِمَطْهَرَةٍ - يَعْنِي: إِدَاوَةً - فَوَجَدَهُ سَاجِدًا فِي شَرَبَةٍ، فَتَنَحَّىٰ
عُمَرُ فَجَلَسَ وَرَاءَهُ حَتَّىٰ رَفَعَ رَأْسَهُ قَالَ: فَقَالَ: «أَحْسَنْتَ يَا عُمَرُ حِينَ
وَجَدْتَنِي سَاجِدًا فَتَنَحَّيْتَ عَنِّي؛ إِنَّ جِبْرِيلَ عَلَيْهِ السَّلَامُ أَتَانِي فَقَالَ: مَنْ
صَلَّىٰ عَلَيْكَ وَاحِدَةً صَلَّى اللهُ عَلَيْهِ عَشْرًا، وَرَفَعَهُ عَشْرَ دَرَجَاتٍ».

4. Anas b. Mālik ؓ reported: "Once, Allāh's Messenger ﷺ set out to relieve himself and did not find anyone to follow him. ʿUmar hurriedly followed him and brought a leather flask that is used for purification. He found him prostrating in a *sharabah*²⁷. ʿUmar withdrew and sat behind him until he lifted his head, and [the Prophet ﷺ] said, **'You have done well, ʿUmar, when you found me prostrating and withdrew away from me. Jibrīl ؑ came to me and said, 'Whoever sends one *ṣalāt* upon you, Allāh will send ten *ṣalāt* upon them and will raise them tenfold in rank.'"²⁸**

---

25 [T] In the printed edition, it states, "Let one," but what I have placed is correct, as stated by Asʿad Tayyim.
26 Reported by al-Bayhaqī in *Shuʿab al-Īmān* (1559) and others. Although this particular chain of narration is weak, when accounting for its supporting narrations, its meaning can ascend to a *ḥasan* grade, as stated by al-Imām al-Mundhirī in *al-Targhīb wa 'l-Tarhīb* (2/500).
27 Al-Shaykh al-Albānī remarked, "It refers to a land filled with herbage but no trees. Refer to *al-Qāmūs*."
28 Reported by al-Bukhārī with similar wording in *al-Adab al-Mufrad* (642), and al-Albānī graded al-Bukhārī's chain of narration as *ḥasan*. The chain of

٥ - حَدَّثَنَا يَعقُوبُ بْنُ حُمَيْدٍ، حَدَّثَنِي أَنَسُ بْنُ عِيَاضٍ، عَنْ سَلَمَةَ بْنِ وَرْدَانَ، حَدَّثنِي مَالِكُ بْنُ أَوْسِ بْنِ الْحَدَثَانِ، عَنْ عُمَرَ بْنِ الْخَطَّابِ، قَالَ: خَرَجَ النَّبِيُّ ﷺ يَتبَرَّزُ فَاتَّبَعْتُهُ بِإِدَاوَةٍ مِن ماءٍ فَوَجَدْتُهُ قَدْ فَرَغَ وَوَجَدْتُهُ سَاجِدًا لِلَّهِ فِي شَرَبَةٍ، فَتَنَحَّيْتُ عَنْهُ، فَلَمَّا فَرَغَ، رَفَعَ رَأْسَهُ فَقَالَ: «**أَحْسَنْتَ يَا عُمَرُ حِينَ تَنَحَّيْتَ عَنِّي، إِنَّ جِبْرِيلَ أَتَانِي فَقَالَ: مَنْ صَلَّىٰ عَلَيْكَ صَلَاةً، صَلَّىٰ اللهُ عَلَيْهِ عَشْرًا، وَرَفَعَهُ عَشْرَ دَرَجَاتٍ**».

5. ʿUmar b. al-Khaṭṭāb ؓ reported: "Once, Allāh's Messenger ﷺ set out to relieve himself, and I followed him with a leather flask [filled with water.][29] I found that he had already completed relieving himself, and found him prostrating in a *sharabah*. When I saw that, I withdrew from him. When he finished, he raised his head and said, **'You have done well, ʿUmar, when you found me prostrating and withdrew away from me. Jibrīl came to me and said, "Whoever sends one *ṣalāt* upon you, Allāh will send ten *ṣalāt* upon them and will raise them tenfold in rank."'"**[30]

٦ - حَدَّثَنَا عَاصِمُ بْنُ عَلِيٍّ، قَالَ: ثنا شُعْبَةُ بْنُ الْحَجَّاجِ، عَنْ عَاصِمِ بْنِ عُبَيْدِ اللهِ، عَنْ عَبْدِ اللهِ بْنِ عَامِرِ بْنِ رَبِيعَةَ، عَنْ أَبِيهِ قَالَ: سَمِعْتُ النَّبِيَّ ﷺ يَقُولُ: «**مَا مِنْ عَبْدٍ يُصَلِّي عَلَيَّ إِلَّا صَلَّتْ عَلَيْهِ الْمَلَائِكَةُ مَا صَلَّىٰ عَلَيَّ،**

---

narration of the author is weak, however, as one of the narrators, Salamah b. Wardān, was declared weak by the great critics of ḥadīth, including al-Imām Aḥmad b. Ḥanbal, Abū Ḥātim al-Rāzī, Abū Dāwūd al-Sijistānī, Yaḥyā b. Maʿīn, and others.

29 [T] This was missing in the text.

30 Ibid.

«فَلْيُقِلَّ مِنْ ذَلِكَ أَوْ لِيُكْثِرْ».

6. Rabīʿah b. Kaʿb ؓ reported: I heard the Prophet ﷺ say: **"There is not a slave that sends ṣalāt upon me except that the angels continuously send ṣalāt upon them, for the duration they are sending ṣalāt upon me. Therefore, let one do so often, or infrequently."**[31]

٧ – حَدَّثَنَا يَحْيَىٰ بْنُ عَبْدِ الْحَمِيدِ، قَالَ: ثنا عَبْدُ الْعَزِيزِ بْنُ مُحَمَّدٍ، عَنْ عَمْرِو بْنِ أَبِي عمرو، عَنْ عَبْدِ الْوَاحِدِ بْنِ مُحَمَّدٍ، عَنْ عَبْدِ الرَّحْمَنِ بْنِ عَوْفٍ قَالَ: أَتَيْتُ النَّبِيَّ ﷺ وَهُوَ سَاجِدٌ فَأَطَالَ السُّجُودَ، قَالَ: «أَتَانِي جِبْرِيلُ قَالَ: مَنْ صَلَّىٰ عَلَيْكَ صَلَّيْتُ عَلَيْهِ، وَمَنْ سَلَّمَ عَلَيْكَ سَلَّمْتُ عَلَيْهِ، فَسَجَدْتُ لِلَّهِ شُكْرًا».

7. ʿAbd al-Raḥmān b. ʿAwf ؓ reported: "I approached the Prophet ﷺ while he was prostrating. He prolonged his prostration and then said, **'Jibrīl came to me and said, "Whoever sends ṣalāt upon you, I send ṣalāt upon them, and whoever sends salām upon you, I send salām upon them." So, I prostrated to Allāh to**

---

31 Al-Albānī said, "This was reported by Aḥmad [15689], Ibn Abī Shaybah, Ibn Mājah (907), and others via the route of ʿĀṣim b. ʿUbaydillāh. Al-Mundhirī said in *al-Targhīb* (2/280), 'Although ʿĀṣim is weak in ḥadīth, some have accepted his narrations, and al-Tirmidhī authenticated a report through him. This ḥadīth is *ḥasan* when considering its supporting narrations, and Allāh knows best.' This ḥadīth is also corroborated by ḥadīth number 3 in this very book. I also found that it was reported with a corroborating chain of narration by Abū Nuʿaym in *al-Ḥilyah* (1/180). Therefore, at worst, it is of *ḥasan* grade."

thank Him.'"[32]

٨ – حَدَّثَنَا أَبُو ثَابِتٍ قَالَ: ثنا عَبْدُ الْعَزِيزِ بْنُ أَبِي حَازِمٍ، عَنِ الْعَلَاءِ بْنِ عَبْدِ الرَّحْمَنِ، عَنْ أَبِيهِ، عَنْ أَبِي هُرَيْرَةَ: أَنَّ رَسُولَ اللهِ ﷺ قَالَ: **«مَنْ صَلَّى عَلَيَّ، صَلَّى اللهُ عَلَيْهِ عَشْرًا»**.

8. Abū Hurayrah ﵁ reported that Allāh's Messenger ﷺ said: **"Whoever sends *ṣalāt* upon me, Allāh the Exalted sends ten *ṣalāt* upon them."**[33]

٩ – حَدَّثَنَا عِيسَى بْنُ مِينَاءٍ قَالَ: ثنا مُحَمَّدُ بْنُ جَعْفَرٍ، عَنِ الْعَلَاءِ، عَنْ أَبِيهِ، عَنْ أَبِي هُرَيْرَةَ، أَنَّ رَسُولَ اللهِ ﷺ قَالَ: **«مَنْ صَلَّى عَلَيَّ وَاحِدَةً، صَلَّى اللهُ عَلَيْهِ عَشْرًا»**.

9. Abū Hurayrah ﵁ reported that Allāh's Messenger ﷺ said: **"Whoever sends one *ṣalāt* upon me, Allāh the Exalted sends ten *ṣalāt* upon them."**[34]

١٠ – حَدَّثَنَا عَلِيُّ بْنُ عَبْدِ اللهِ قَالَ: ثنا زَيْدُ بْنُ الْحُبَابِ، حَدَّثَنِي مُوسَى بْنُ عُبَيْدَةَ قَالَ: أَخْبَرَنِي قَيْسُ بْنُ عَبْدِ الرَّحْمَنِ بْنِ أَبِي صَعْصَعَةَ، عَنْ سَعْدِ بْنِ إِبْرَاهِيمَ، عَنْ أَبِيهِ، عَنْ جَدِّهِ عَبْدِ الرَّحْمَنِ بْنِ عَوْفٍ قَالَ: كَانَ لَا يُفَارِقُ فَيْءَ النَّبِيِّ ﷺ بِاللَّيْلِ وَالنَّهَارِ خَمْسَةُ نَفَرٍ مِنْ أَصْحَابِهِ أَوْ أَرْبَعَةٌ لِمَا يَنُوبُهُ مِنْ

32 Reported by Aḥmad (1665) and al-Ḥākim (2019) who judged the *ḥadīth* to be authentic.
33 Reported by al-Imām Muslim (408).
34 Reported by Aḥmad (8637) and it is authentic.

حَوَائِجِهِ. قَالَ: فَجِئْتُ فَوَجَدْتُهُ قَدْ خَرَجَ فَتَبِعْتُهُ، فَدَخَلَ حَائِطًا مِنْ حِيطَانِ الْأَسْوَافِ، فَصَلَّىٰ فَسَجَدَ سَجْدَةً أَطَالَ فِيهَا، فَحَزِنْتُ وَبَكَيْتُ فَقُلْتُ: لَأَرَىٰ رَسُولَ اللهِ ﷺ قَدْ قَبَضَ اللهُ رُوحَهُ قَالَ: فَرَفَعَ رَأْسَهُ وَتَرَاءَيْتُ لَهُ فَدَعَانِي فَقَالَ: «**مَا لَكَ؟**»

10. 'Abd al-Raḥmān b. 'Awf ﷺ reported, "There were four or five companions who never parted from the shadow of the Prophet ﷺ during the day and night, who would fulfil his needs. I approached him and found that he had already left, so I followed him. He entered one of the enclosed gardens of al-Aswāf[35] and prayed therein. He offered a very long prostration which caused me to become saddened and begin to cry. I thought to myself, 'Surely, I see that Allāh has taken the soul of Allāh's Messenger ﷺ.' Then, he lifted his head and I made myself visible to him. He called me to come to him and said, **'What is wrong with you?'**

قُلْتُ: يَا رَسُولَ اللهِ سَجَدْتَ سَجْدَةً أَطَلْتَ فِيهَا فَحَزِنْتُ وَبَكَيْتُ وَقُلْتُ: لَأَرَىٰ رَسُولَ اللهِ ﷺ قَدْ قَبَضَ اللهُ رُوحَهُ.

I responded, 'Messenger of Allāh, I saw you offer a very long prostration, so I became sad and cried, thinking that Allāh had taken the soul of Allāh's Messenger ﷺ.'

قَالَ: «**هَذِهِ سَجْدَةٌ سَجَدْتُهَا شُكْرًا لِرَبِّي فِيمَا آتَانِي فِي أُمَّتِي، مَنْ صَلَّىٰ عَلَيَّ صَلَاةً كَتَبَ اللهُ لَهُ عَشْرَ حَسَنَاتٍ**».

35 Al-Aswaf refers to the sanctuary of al-Madīnah which was sanctified by Allāh's Messenger ﷺ.

He replied, **'I offered that prostration in thanks to my Lord for what He has bestowed upon me among my Ummah, for if one sends one *ṣalāt* upon me, Allāh writes ten good deeds for them.'"**[36]

١١ - حَدَّثَنَا مُسَدَّدٌ قَالَ: ثنا بِشْرُ بْنُ الْمُفَضَّلِ، قَالَ: ثنا عَبْدُ الرَّحْمَنِ بْنُ إِسْحَاقَ، عَنِ الْعَلَاءِ بْنِ عَبْدِ الرَّحْمَنِ، عَنْ أَبِيهِ، عَنْ أَبِي هُرَيْرَةَ قَالَ: قَالَ: رَسُولُ اللهِ ﷺ: «مَنْ صَلَّىٰ عَلَيَّ مَرَّةً وَاحِدَةً كَتَبَ اللهُ لَهُ عَشْرَ حَسَنَاتٍ».

11. Abū Hurayrah ﵁ reported that Allāh's Messenger ﷺ said, **"Whoever sends *ṣalāt* upon me once, Allāh writes ten good deeds for them."**[37]

١٢ - حَدَّثَنَا عَبْدُ الرَّحْمَنِ بْنُ وَاقِدٍ الْعَطَّارُ قَالَ: ثنا هُشَيْمٌ قَالَ: ثنا الْعَوَّامُ بْنُ حَوْشَبٍ، حَدَّثَنِي رَجُلٌ مِنْ بَنِي أَسَدٍ، عَنْ عَبْدِ الرَّحْمَنِ بْنِ عَمْرٍو قَالَ: «مَنْ صَلَّىٰ عَلَىٰ النَّبِيِّ ﷺ كَتَبَ اللهُ لَهُ عَشْرَ حَسَنَاتٍ وَمَحَا عَنْهُ عَشْرَ سَيِّئَاتٍ وَرَفَعَ لَهُ عَشْرَ دَرَجَاتٍ».

12. 'Abd al-Raḥmān b. 'Amr ﵁ said: "Whoever sends *ṣalāt* upon the Prophet ﷺ, Allāh writes ten good deeds for them, erases ten sins, and raises them ten levels."[38]

---

36 Reported by Ibn Abī Shaybah in *al-Muṣannaf* (2/517), and like the previous ḥadīth, it is authentic due to its supporting narrations.

37 Reported by Aḥmad (7508) and al-Haythamī judged the ḥadīth as authentic.

38 Al-Albānī said, "This chain of narration is weak as a *mawqūf* report (i.e. attributed to the companion), but it has *marfu'* (i.e. attributed to the Prophet

١٣ - حَدَّثَنَا عَلِيُّ بْنُ عَبْدِ اللهِ، قَالَ: ثنا سُفْيَانُ، عَنْ يَعْقُوبَ بْنِ زَيْدِ بْنِ طَلْحَةَ التَّيْمِيِّ، قَالَ: قَالَ رَسُولُ اللهِ ﷺ: «أَتَانِي آتٍ مِنْ رَبِّي فَقَالَ: مَا مِنْ عَبْدٍ يُصَلِّي عَلَيْكَ صَلَاةً إِلَّا صَلَّى اللهُ عَلَيْهِ بِهَا عَشْرًا». فَقَامَ إِلَيْهِ رَجُلٌ فَقَالَ: يَا رَسُولَ اللهِ أَجْعَلُ نِصْفَ دُعَائِي لَكَ؟ قَالَ: «إِنْ شِئْتَ»، قَالَ: أَلَا أَجْعَلُ ثُلُثَيْ دُعَائِي لَكَ؟ قَالَ: «إِنْ شِئْتَ»، قَالَ: أَلَا أَجْعَلُ دُعَائِي لَكَ كُلَّهُ؟ قَالَ: «إِذَنْ يَكْفِيكَ اللهُ هَمَّ الدُّنْيَا، وَهَمَّ الْآخِرَةِ».

13. Yaʿqūb b. Zayd b. Ṭalḥah al-Taymī reported that Allāh's Messenger ﷺ said: **"A messenger came to me from my Lord and informed me, 'There is not a slave who sends a single ṣalāt upon you but that Allāh sends ten ṣalāt upon them.'"** Then, a man approached him and said, "Messenger of Allāh, should I make half of my supplications for you?" He replied, **"If you wish."** He then said, "Shall I not make two-thirds of my supplications for you?" [The Prophet ﷺ] replied, **"If you so wish."** The man said, "Shall I not make all of my supplications for you?" He ﷺ replied, **"If you do so, Allāh will quell your worries in the worldly life and your worries in the hereafter."**[39]

قَالَ شَيْخٌ كَانَ بِمَكَّةَ يُقَالُ لَهُ مَنِيعٌ لِسُفْيَانَ: عَمَّنْ أَسْنَدَهُ؟ قَالَ: لَا أَدْرِي.

A *shaykh* in Makkah named Maniʿ said to Sufyān, "Who did [Yaʿqub b. Zayd] attribute this narration to?" [Sufyān] replied, "I do not

ﷺ) supporting narrations from Anas ؓ, reported by al-Nasāʾī and others, with an authentic chain of narration."

39 Al-Albānī said, "This chain of narration is authentic, though *mursal* (meaning, the companion's name was omitted). However, it is supported by the next narration mentioned."

know."

١٤ - حَدَّثَنَا سَعِيدُ بْنُ سَلَّامٍ الْعَطَّارُ، قَالَ: ثنا سُفْيَانُ - يَعْنِي الثَّوْرِيَّ - عَنْ عَبْدِ اللهِ بْنِ مُحَمَّدِ بْنِ عَقِيلٍ، عَنِ الطُّفَيْلِ بْنِ أُبَيِّ بْنِ كَعْبٍ، عَنْ أَبِيهِ قَالَ: كَانَ رَسُولُ اللهِ ﷺ يَخْرُجُ فِي ثُلُثِ اللَّيْلِ فَيَقُولُ: «**جَاءَتِ الرَّاجِفَةُ تَتْبَعُهَا الرَّادِفَةُ، جَاءَ الْمَوْتُ بِمَا فِيهِ**»، وَقَالَ أُبَيٌّ: يَا رَسُولَ اللهِ إِنِّي أُصَلِّي مِنَ اللَّيْلِ أَفَأَجْعَلُ لَكَ ثُلُثَ صَلَاتِي؟ قَالَ رَسُولُ اللهِ ﷺ: «**الشَّطْرُ**» قَالَ: أَفَأَجْعَلُ لَكَ شَطْرَ صَلَاتِي؟ قَالَ رَسُولُ اللهِ ﷺ «**الثُّلُثَانِ أَكْثَرُ**»، قَالَ: أَفَأَجْعَلُ لَكَ صَلَاتِي كُلَّهَا؟ قَالَ: «**إِذَنْ يُغْفَرُ لَكَ ذَنْبُكَ كُلُّهُ**».

14. Ubayy b. Kaʿb reported that Allāh's Messenger ﷺ used to set out in the third of the night and would say, **"The shocking event is nigh, followed by the second blast [of the blowing of the trumpet]. Death is approaching with all it entails."** Ubayy said, "Messenger of Allāh, I pray by night; shall I dedicate a third of my supplications for you?" Allāh's Messenger ﷺ replied, "**Nay, but half.**" Ubayy said, "Then shall I dedicate half of my supplications for you?" Allāh's Messenger ﷺ said, "**But two-thirds is more.**" He replied, "Shall I dedicate all of my supplications to you?" He said, "**If you do so, all of your sins will be forgiven.**"[40]

١٥ - حَدَّثَنَا عَبْدُ اللهِ بْنُ مَسْلَمَةَ قَالَ: ثنا سَلَمَةُ بْنُ وَرْدَانَ قَالَ: سَمِعْتُ

---

40 Al-Albānī said, "It was reported by al-Tirmidhī [2457] who said it was of the grade *ḥasan ṣaḥīḥ*." It was also reported by al-Ḥākim in *al-Mustadrak* (3578) who said, "This ḥadīth has an authentic chain of narration, but [the Two *Shaykhs*] did not report it."

أَنَسَ بْنَ مَالِكٍ، يَقُولُ: ارْتَقَىٰ النَّبِيُّ ﷺ عَلَى الْمِنْبَرِ دَرَجَةً فَقَالَ: «آمِينَ»، ثُمَّ ارْتَقَىٰ الثَّانِيَةَ فَقَالَ: «آمِينَ»، ثُمَّ ارْتَقَىٰ الثَّالِثَةَ فَقَالَ: «آمِينَ»، ثُمَّ اسْتَوَىٰ فَجَلَسَ، فَقَالَ أَصْحَابُهُ: عَلَىٰ مَا أَمَّنْتَ؟ قَالَ: «أَتَانِي جِبْرِيلُ فَقَالَ: رَغِمَ أَنْفُ امْرِئٍ ذُكِرْتَ عِنْدَهُ فَلَمْ يُصَلِّ عَلَيْكَ، فَقُلْتُ: آمِينَ، فَقَالَ: رَغِمَ أَنْفُ امْرِئٍ أَدْرَكَ أَبَوَيْهِ فَلَمْ يَدْخُلِ الْجَنَّةَ، فَقُلْتُ: آمِينَ، فَقَالَ: رَغِمَ أَنْفُ امْرِئٍ أَدْرَكَ رَمَضَانَ فَلَمْ يُغْفَرْ لَهُ فَقُلْتُ: آمِينَ».

15. Anas b. Mālik said: "The Prophet ﷺ ascended a step of the pulpit and said, '**Āmīn (Allāh, answer the supplication).**' Then, he ascended the second step and said, '**Āmīn.**' Then, he ascended the third step and said, '**Āmīn.**' His companions said to him, 'What did you say *āmīn* for?' He replied, '**Jibrīl came to me and said, "Wretched is the person in whose presence you are mentioned yet they send no *ṣalāt* upon you," and I said, "Āmīn." Then, he said, "Wretched is the person who lives to see their parents and does not enter paradise," to which I said, "Āmīn." Then, he said, "Wretched is the person who reaches Ramaḍān but is not forgiven," and I said, "Āmīn."**[41]

١٦ - حَدَّثَنَا مُسَدَّدٌ قَالَ: ثنا بِشْرُ بْنُ الْمُفَضَّلِ قَالَ: ثنا عَبْدُ الرَّحْمَنِ بْنُ إِسْحَاقَ، عَنْ سَعِيدٍ الْمَقْبُرِيِّ، عَنْ أَبِي هُرَيْرَةَ قَالَ: قَالَ رَسُولُ اللهِ ﷺ: «رَغِمَ أَنْفُ رَجُلٍ ذُكِرْتُ عِنْدَهُ فَلَمْ يُصَلِّ عَلَيَّ، وَرَغِمَ أَنْفُ رَجُلٍ أَدْرَكَ

---

41 Al-Albānī said, "This is an authentic ḥadīth when taking its supporting narrations into account. It was reported by Ibn Māsī in *al-Fawā'id* [2] with this wording."

أَبَوَيْهِ عِنْدَ الْكِبَرِ فَلَمْ يُدْخِلَاهُ الْجَنَّةَ، وَرَغِمَ أَنْفُ رَجُلٍ دَخَلَ عَلَيْهِ رَمَضَانُ ثُمَّ انْسَلَخَ قَبْلَ أَنْ يُغْفَرَ لَهُ».

16. Abū Hurayrah ﷺ reported that Allāh's Messenger ﷺ said, **"Wretched is a man in whose presence I am mentioned yet they send no ṣalāt upon me. Wretched is a man who lives to see his parents reach old age yet they do not cause him to enter paradise. Wretched is the man who, Ramaḍān begins while they are alive, yet it ends without them earning forgiveness."**[42]

١٧ - حَدَّثَنَا الْمُقَدَّمِيُّ قَالَ: ثنا يَزِيدُ بْنُ زُرَيْعٍ قَالَ: ثنا عَبْدُ الرَّحْمَنِ بْنُ إِسْحَاقَ، بِإِسْنَادِهِ نَحْوَهُ.

17. We have reported the previous ḥadīth through another chain of narration as well.

١٨ - حَدَّثَنَا أَبُو ثَابِتٍ قَالَ: ثنا عَبْدُ الْعَزِيزِ بْنُ أَبِي حَازِمٍ، عَنْ كَثِيرِ بْنِ زَيْدٍ، عَنِ الْوَلِيدِ بْنِ رَبَاحٍ، عَنْ أَبِي هُرَيْرَةَ: أَنَّ رَسُولَ اللهِ ﷺ رَقِيَ الْمِنْبَرَ فَقَالَ: «آمِينَ آمِينَ آمِينَ»، فَقِيلَ لَهُ: يَا رَسُولَ اللهِ مَا كُنْتَ تَصْنَعُ هَذَا؟ فَقَالَ: «قَالَ لِي جِبْرِيلُ: رَغِمَ أَنْفُ عَبْدٍ دَخَلَ عَلَيْهِ رَمَضَانُ لَمْ يُغْفَرْ لَهُ، فَقُلْتُ: آمِينَ، ثُمَّ قَالَ: رَغِمَ أَنْفُ عَبْدٍ أَدْرَكَ أَبَوَيْهِ أَوْ أَحَدَهُمَا لَمْ يُدْخِلَاهُ الْجَنَّةَ، فَقُلْتُ: آمِينَ ثُمَّ قَالَ: رَغِمَ أَنْفُ عَبْدٍ ذُكِرْتَ عِنْدَهُ فَلَمْ يُصَلِّ عَلَيْكَ، فَقُلْتُ: آمِينَ».

18. Abū Hurayrah ﷺ reported that Allāh's Messenger ﷺ ascend-

---

[42] Reported by Aḥmad (7451) and al-Tirmidhī (3545) and it is an authentic narration, as stated by al-Albānī and al-Arnā'ūṭ.

ed the pulpit and said: ***"Āmīn, Āmīn, Āmīn."*** It was said to him, "Messenger of Allāh, you have never done this before." He replied, **"Jibrīl told me, 'Wretched is the slave who, Ramaḍān begins while they are alive but they are not forgiven,' so I said, *'Āmīn.'* Then, he said, 'Wretched is a man who lives to see both or one of their parents yet they do not cause him to enter paradise,' so I said, *'Āmīn.'* He then said, 'Wretched is the person in whose presence you are mentioned yet they send no *ṣalāt* upon you,' and I said, *'Āmīn.'*"**[43]

١٩ - حَدَّثَنَا مُحَمَّدُ بْنُ إِسْحَاقَ قَالَ: ثنا ابْنُ أَبِي مَرْيَمَ قَالَ: ثنا مُحَمَّدُ بْنُ هِلَالٍ، حَدَّثَنِي سَعْدُ بْنُ إِسْحَاقَ بْنِ كَعْبِ بْنِ عُجْرَةَ، عَنْ أَبِيهِ، عَنْ كَعْبِ بْنِ عُجْرَةَ قَالَ: قَالَ رَسُولُ اللهِ ﷺ: «**احْضُرُوا الْمِنْبَرَ**» فَحَضَرْنَا فَلَمَّا ارْتَقَى الدَّرَجَةَ قَالَ: «**آمِينَ**»، ثُمَّ ارْتَقَى الدَّرَجَةَ الثَّانِيَةَ فَقَالَ: «**آمِينَ**» ثُمَّ ارْتَقَى الدَّرَجَةَ الثَّالِثَةَ فَقَالَ: «**آمِينَ**».

19. Ka'b b. 'Ujrah ﵁ said: "Allāh's Messenger ﷺ said, **'Attend the pulpit,'** which we did. When he climbed the first step [of the pulpit], he said ***'Āmīn* (Allāh, answer the supplication).'** Then, he ascended the second step and said, ***'Āmīn.'*** Then, he ascended the third step and said, ***'Āmīn.'***

فَلَمَّا فَرَغَ نَزَلَ عَنِ الْمِنْبَرِ قَالَ: فَقُلْنَا لَهُ: يَا رَسُولَ اللهِ لَقَدْ سَمِعْنَا مِنْكَ الْيَوْمَ شَيْئًا مَا كُنَّا نَسْمَعُهُ قَالَ: «**إِنَّ جِبْرِيلَ عَرَضَ لِي فَقَالَ: بَعُدَ مَنْ أَدْرَكَ رَمَضَانَ**

43 Al-Albānī said, "It has a *ḥasan* chain of narration." It was also reported by Ibn Khuzaymah (1888), Ibn Ḥibbān (2028) and al-Bukhārī in *al-Adab al-Mufrad* (646).

فَلَمْ يُغْفَرْ لَهُ فَقُلْتُ: آمِينَ، فَلَمَّا رَقِيتُ الثَّانِيَةَ قَالَ: بَعُدَ مَنْ ذُكِرْتَ عِنْدَهُ فَلَمْ يُصَلِّ عَلَيْكَ فَقُلْتُ: آمِينَ، فَلَمَّا رَقِيتُ الثَّالِثَةَ قَالَ: بَعُدَ مَنْ أَدْرَكَ أَبَوَيْهِ الْكِبَرُ أَوْ أَحَدَهُمَا فَلَمْ يُدْخِلَاهُ الْجَنَّةَ فَقُلْتُ: آمِينَ».

After he finished [his speech], he descended and we said to him, 'Messenger of Allāh, we heard something from you today which we have never heard before.' He replied, **'Jibrīl presented himself to me and said, "Shunned is the one who reaches Ramaḍān but is not forgiven," and I said, "*Āmīn.*" When I ascended the second step, he said, "Shunned is the one in whose presence you are mentioned yet they send no *ṣalāt* upon you," and I said, "*Āmīn.*" Then, when I took the third step, he said, "Shunned is the one who lives to see both or one of their parents yet they do not cause him to enter paradise," and to that, I said, "*Āmīn.*"'"**[44]

٢٠ - حَدَّثَنَا جَعْفَرُ بْنُ إِبْرَاهِيمَ بْنِ مُحَمَّدِ بْنِ عَلِيِّ بْنِ عَبْدِ اللهِ بْنِ جَعْفَرِ بْنِ أَبِي طَالِبٍ، عَمَّنْ أَخْبَرَهُ مِنْ أَهْلِ بَلَدِهِ، عَنْ عَلِيِّ بْنِ حُسَيْنِ بْنِ عَلِيٍّ، أَنَّ رَجُلًا، كَانَ يَأْتِي غَدَاةً فَيَزُورُ قَبْرَ النَّبِيِّ ﷺ وَيُصَلِّي عَلَيْهِ وَيَصْنَعُ مِنْ ذَلِكَ مَا اشْتَهَرَهُ عَلَيْهِ عَلِيُّ بْنُ الْحُسَيْنِ، فَقَالَ لَهُ عَلِيُّ بْنُ الْحُسَيْنِ: مَا يَحْمِلُكَ عَلَىٰ هَذَا؟ قَالَ: أُحِبُّ التَّسْلِيمَ عَلَىٰ النَّبِيِّ ﷺ، فَقَالَ لَهُ عَلِيُّ بْنُ الْحُسَيْنِ: هَلْ لَكَ أَنْ أُحَدِّثَكَ حَدِيثًا عَنْ أَبِي؟ قَالَ: نَعَمْ، فَقَالَ لَهُ عَلِيُّ بْنُ حُسَيْنٍ: أَخْبَرَنِي أَبِي عَنْ جَدِّي أَنَّهُ قَالَ: قَالَ رَسُولُ اللهِ ﷺ: **«لَا تَجْعَلُوا**

44 Reported by al-Ḥākim (7256) who judged it as authentic.

قَبْرِي عِيدًا وَلَا تَجْعَلُوا بُيُوتَكُمْ قُبُورًا، وَصَلُّوا عَلَيَّ وَسَلِّمُوا حَيْثُمَا كُنْتُمْ فَسَيَبْلُغُنِي سَلَامُكُمْ وَصَلَاتُكُمْ».

20. ʿAlī b. al-Ḥusayn b. ʿAlī [b. Abī Ṭālib] reported that a man would visit the grave of the Prophet ﷺ every morning and send *ṣalāt* upon him. He would do the actions that ʿAlī b. al-Ḥusayn later publicised about him. ʿAlī b. al-Ḥusayn said, "What causes you to do this?" The man replied, "I love to send salutations upon the Prophet ﷺ." ʿAlī b. al-Ḥusayn said, "Shall I narrate to you a ḥadīth taught to me by my father?" The man said, "Yes." ʿAlī b. al-Ḥusayn said, "My father narrated to me from my grandfather, who reported that Allāh's Messenger ﷺ said, **'Do not make my grave resemble a celebratory practice[45], and do not make your homes into graves. Send *ṣalāt* upon me and send salutations upon me wherever you are, for your salutations and sending of *ṣalāt* shall reach me.'"**[46]

٢١ - حَدَّثَنَا مُسَدَّدٌ قَالَ: ثنا يَحْيَى، عَنْ سُفْيَانَ، حَدَّثَنِي عَبْدُ اللهِ بْنُ السَّائِبِ، عَنْ زَاذَانَ، عَنْ عَبْدِ اللهِ - هُوَ ابْنُ مَسْعُودٍ - عَنِ النَّبِيِّ ﷺ قَالَ: «إِنَّ لِلَّهِ فِي الْأَرْضِ مَلَائِكَةً سَيَّاحِينَ يُبَلِّغُونِي مِنْ أُمَّتِي السَّلَامَ».

21. ʿAbdullāh b. Masʿūd reported that the Prophet ﷺ said, **"Allāh**

---

45 [T] The word used in Arabic is *ʿid*, which as we all know is the term for a celebration. However, the linguistic meaning of the word is 'Something that often repeats.' Therefore, here the Prophet ﷺ is forbidding people from constantly visiting his grave anytime they wish to send *ṣalāt* upon him. Refer to *Fayḍ al-Qadīr* (4/199).

46 Al-Albānī said, "This is an authentic ḥadīth when considering its supporting narrations." [T] Similar narrations were reported by Aḥmad (8804) and Abū Dāwūd (2042).

has placed angels to traverse the world who inform me when a member of my Ummah sends me salutations."[47]

٢٢ - حَدَّثَنَا عَلِيُّ بْنُ عَبْدِ اللهِ، قَالَ: ثنا حُسَيْنُ بْنُ عَلِيٍّ الْجُعْفِيُّ، قَالَ: ثنا عَبْدُ الرَّحْمَنِ بْنُ يَزِيدَ بْنِ جَابِرٍ، سَمِعْتُهُ يَذْكُرُ، عَنْ أَبِي الْأَشْعَثِ الصَّنْعَانِيِّ، عَنْ أَوْسِ بْنِ أَوْسٍ أَنَّ رَسُولَ اللهِ ﷺ قَالَ: «**إِنَّ مِنْ أَفْضَلِ أَيَّامِكُمْ يَوْمَ الْجُمُعَةِ؛ فِيهِ خُلِقَ آدَمُ، وَفِيهِ قُبِضَ، وَفِيهِ النَّفْخَةُ، وَفِيهِ الصَّعْقَةُ، فَأَكْثِرُوا عَلَيَّ مِنَ الصَّلَاةِ فِيهِ فَإِنَّ صَلَاتَكُمْ مَعْرُوضَةٌ عَلَيَّ**».

22. Aws b. Aws reported that Allāh's Messenger ﷺ said, **"One of your best days is Friday. On that day, Allāh created Adam, and on that day, he was deceased. On that day is the blowing [into the trumpet, causing the start of the Day of Judgement], and on that day is the death [caused by the first blowing of the trumpet]. Therefore, send *ṣalāt* upon me often [on that day]**[48]**, for your *ṣalāt* are presented to me."**

قَالُوا: يَا رَسُولَ اللهِ كَيْفَ تُعْرَضُ عَلَيْكَ صَلَاتُنَا وَقَدْ أَرِمْتَ؟ - يَقُولُونَ: قَدْ بَلِيتَ - قَالَ: «**إِنَّ اللهَ حَرَّمَ عَلَى الْأَرْضِ أَنْ تَأْكُلَ أَجْسَادَ الْأَنْبِيَاءِ**».

[The companions] said, "Messenger of Allāh, how will they be presented to you after you die?" He replied, **"Allāh has forbidden the earth from eating the bodies of the prophets."**[49]

---

47 Reported by Aḥmad (3666) and it has an authentic chain of narration, according to al-Albānī.
48 [T] This was a missing word, as pointed out by Tayyim.
49 Reported by Abū Dāwūd (1047) and Aḥmad (16162). Al-Albānī judged

٢٣ - حَدَّثَنَا سُلَيْمَانُ بْنُ حَرْبٍ، قَالَ: ثنا جَرِيرُ بْنُ حَازِمٍ قَالَ: سَمِعْتُ الْحَسَنَ، يَقُولُ: قَالَ: رَسُولُ اللهِ صَلَّىٰ اللهُ عَلَيْهِ وَسَلَّمَ: «**لَا تَأْكُلُ الْأَرْضُ جَسَدَ مَنْ كَلَّمَهُ رُوحُ الْقُدُسِ**».

23. Al-Ḥasān [al-Baṣrī] said, "Allāh's Messenger ﷺ said, **'The earth does not cause decay to a body spoken to by the Holy Spirit.'**"[50]

٢٤ - حَدَّثَنَا إِبْرَاهِيمُ بْنُ الْحَجَّاجِ، قَالَ: ثنا وُهَيْبٌ، عَنْ أَيُّوبَ، قَالَ: بَلَغَنِي - وَاللهُ أَعْلَمُ - أَنَّ مَلَكًا مُوَكَّلٌ بِكُلِّ مَنْ صَلَّىٰ عَلَىٰ النَّبِيِّ ﷺ حَتَّىٰ يُبَلِّغَهُ النَّبِيَّ ﷺ.

24. Ayyūb said, "I was informed, and Allāh knows best, that there is an angel designated specifically to the one who sends *ṣalāt* upon the Prophet ﷺ and conveys it to the Prophet ﷺ."[51]

٢٥ - حَدَّثَنَا سُلَيْمَانُ بْنُ حَرْبٍ، قَالَ: ثنا حَمَّادُ بْنُ زَيْدٍ قَالَ: ثنا غَالِبٌ الْقَطَّانُ، عَنْ بَكْرِ بْنِ عَبْدِ اللهِ الْمُزَنِيِّ: قَالَ رَسُولُ اللهِ ﷺ: «**حَيَاتِي خَيْرٌ لَكُمْ، تُحَدِّثُونَ وَيُحَدَّثُ لَكُمْ، فَإِذَا أَنَا مُتُّ كَانَتْ وَفَاتِي خَيْرًا لَكُمْ، تُعْرَضُ عَلَيَّ أَعْمَالُكُمْ فَإِنْ رَأَيْتُ خَيْرًا حَمِدْتُ اللهَ، وَإِنْ رَأَيْتُ غَيْرَ ذَلِكَ اسْتَغْفَرْتُ**

---

its chain of narration as authentic.

50 Al-Albānī said, "This is an authentic ḥadīth, as it is corroborated by the previous ḥadīth. The chain of narration is authentic, though *mursal*, as al-Ḥasan is al-Baṣrī (who was one of the Tābiʿīn) is present."

51 Al-Albānī said, "The chain of narration is authentic up to Ayyub al-Sakhtiyānī, and it can be attributed to the Prophet ﷺ because such a thing cannot be uttered out of conjecture."

اللهَ لَكُمْ».

25. Bakr b. ʿAbdillāh al-Muzanī said, "Allāh's Messenger ﷺ said, '**My life is goodness for you. You commit errors, and rulings are communicated to you. However, when I pass away, my death shall be goodness for you. Your actions will be presented to me. If I see goodness, I shall praise Allāh, and if I see anything else, I shall ask Allāh to forgive you.**'"[52]

٢٦ - حَدَّثَنَا الْحَجَّاجُ بْنُ الْمِنْهَالِ قَالَ: ثنا حَمَّادُ بْنُ سَلَمَةَ، عَنْ كَثِيرٍ أَبِي الْفَضْلِ، عَنْ بَكْرِ بْنِ عَبْدِ اللهِ، أَنَّ رَسُولَ اللهِ ﷺ قَالَ: «حَيَاتِي خَيْرٌ لَكُمْ، وَوَفَاتِي لَكُمْ خَيْرٌ، تُحَدِّثُونَ فَيُحَدَّثُ لَكُمْ فَإِذَا أَنَا مُتُّ عُرِضَتْ عَلَيَّ أَعْمَالُكُمْ، فَإِنْ رَأَيْتُ خَيْرًا حَمِدْتُ اللهَ، وَإِنْ رَأَيْتُ شَرًّا اسْتَغْفَرْتُ اللهَ لَكُمْ».

26. Bakr b. ʿAbdillāh reported that Allāh's Messenger ﷺ said, "**My life is goodness for you, and my death shall be goodness for you. You commit errors, and rulings are communicated to you. When I pass away, your actions will be presented to me. If I see goodness, I shall praise Allāh, and if I see anything else, I shall ask Allāh to forgive you.**"[53]

52 Al-Albānī said, "This chain of narration is authentic [up until Bakr b. ʿAbdillāh], but is *mursal*." [T] Al-ʿIrāqī said in his *Takhrīj Iḥyāʾ ʿUlūm al-Dīn* (5/2190), "It was reported by al-Bazzār via ʿAbdullāh b. Masʿūd, and its narrators are all those in the *Ṣaḥīḥ* collections, except for ʿAbd al-Majīd b. ʿAbd al-ʿAzīz b. [Abī] Rawwād. Although Muslim reported through him, and Ibn Maʿīn and al-Nasāʾī judged him to be trustworthy, others have declared him weak."

53 Al-Albānī remarked, "This is another chain of narration up until Bakr b.

٢٧ - حَدَّثَنَا عَبْدُ الرَّحْمَنِ بْنُ وَاقِدٍ الْعَطَّارُ قَالَ: ثنا هُشَيْمٌ، قَالَ: ثنا حُصَيْنُ بْنُ عَبْدِ الرَّحْمَنِ، عَنْ يَزِيدَ الرَّقَاشِيِّ: أَنَّ مَلَكًا مُوَكَّلٌ يَوْمَ الْجُمُعَةِ مَنْ صَلَّىٰ عَلَىٰ النَّبِيِّ ﷺ يُبَلِّغُ النَّبِيَّ ﷺ، يَقُولُ: إِنَّ فُلَانًا مِنْ أُمَّتِكَ صَلَّىٰ عَلَيْكَ.

27. Yazīd al-Raqqāshī said, "There is an angel designated on Friday. Whoever sends *ṣalāt* upon the Prophet ﷺ, [that angel] informs the Prophet ﷺ, and says, 'So-and-so person of your Ummah has sent *ṣalāt* upon you.'"[54]

٢٨ - حَدَّثَنَا مُسْلِمٌ قَالَ: ثنا مُبَارَكٌ، عَنِ الْحَسَنِ، عَنِ النَّبِيِّ ﷺ قَالَ: «**أَكْثِرُوا عَلَيَّ الصَّلَاةَ يَوْمَ الْجُمُعَةِ**».

28. Mubārak b. al-Ḥasan reported that the Prophet ﷺ said, **"Send abundant *ṣalāt* upon me on Fridays."**[55]

٢٩ - حَدَّثَنَا سَلْمُ بْنُ سُلَيْمَانَ الضَّبِّيُّ قَالَ: ثنا أَبُو حُرَّةَ، عَنِ الْحَسَنِ، قَالَ: قَالَ رَسُولُ اللهِ ﷺ: «**أَكْثِرُوا عَلَيَّ الصَّلَاةَ يَوْمَ الْجُمُعَةِ فَإِنَّهَا تُعْرَضُ عَلَيَّ**».

29. Al-Ḥasan reported that Allāh's Messenger ﷺ said, **"Send abundant *ṣalāt* upon me on Fridays, for they are presented to me."**[56]

'Abdillāh, and it is a great chain of narration."

54 Al-Albānī said, "The chain of narration is weak, and ḥadīth number 21 in this very book would serve the same purpose."

55 [T] Reported by 'Abd al-Razzāq (5338) and al-Ṭabarānī in *Musnad al-Shāmiyyīn* (2610), though through Anas b. Mālik ؓ. Shaykh al-Albānī remarked, "It is an authentic ḥadīth, as testified to by narration 22 in this very book."

56 [T] This is a *mursal* narration but attested to by various authentic narrations with similar wordings, such as narration 22 of this very book.

٣٠ - حَدَّثَنَا إِبْرَاهِيمُ بْنُ حَمْزَةَ، قَالَ: ثنا عَبْدُ الْعَزِيزِ بْنُ مُحَمَّدٍ، عَنْ سُهَيْلٍ قَالَ: جِئْتُ أُسَلِّمُ عَلَى النَّبِيِّ ﷺ وَحَسَنُ بْنُ حَسَنٍ يَتَعَشَّى فِي بَيْتٍ عِنْدَ النَّبِيِّ ﷺ، فَدَعَانِي فَجِئْتُهُ فَقَالَ: ادْنُ فَتَعَشَّ، قَالَ: قُلْتُ: لَا أُرِيدُهُ، قَالَ: مَالِي رَأَيْتُكَ وَقَفْتَ؟ قَالَ: وَقَفْتُ أُسَلِّمُ عَلَى النَّبِيِّ ﷺ، قَالَ: إِذَا دَخَلْتَ الْمَسْجِدَ فَسَلِّمْ عَلَيْهِ، ثُمَّ قَالَ: إِنَّ رَسُولَ اللهِ ﷺ قَالَ: «**صَلُّوا فِي بُيُوتِكُمْ وَلَا تَجْعَلُوا بُيُوتَكُمْ مَقَابِرَ، لَعَنَ اللهُ يَهُودَ، اتَّخَذُوا قُبُورَ أَنْبِيَائِهِمْ مَسَاجِدَ، وَصَلُّوا عَلَيَّ؛ فَإِنَّ صَلَاتَكُمْ تَبْلُغُنِي حَيْثُمَا كُنْتُمْ**».

30. Suhayl reported, "I went to give salutations to the Prophet ﷺ and Ḥasan b. Ḥasan was eating dinner in a house near the Prophet ﷺ. He called me over, and I went to him. He said to me, 'Come and eat dinner.' I replied, 'I do not wish to.' He said, 'Why do I see you standing?' I said, 'I stood to give salutations to the Prophet ﷺ.' He said, 'If you enter the mosque, give your salutations,' and then said, 'Allāh's Messenger ﷺ said, **'Pray in your homes; do not make your homes into graves. Curse of Allāh be upon the Jews, for they took the graves of their prophets as places of prayer. Send *ṣalāt* upon me, for your *ṣalāt* reaches me no matter where you are.'"**[57]

٣١ - حَدَّثَنَا إِسْمَاعِيلُ بْنُ أَبِي أُوَيْسٍ، حَدَّثَنِي أَخِي، عَنْ سُلَيْمَانَ بْنِ بِلَالٍ، عَنْ عَمْرِو بْنِ أَبِي عَمْرٍو، عَنْ عَلِيِّ بْنِ حُسَيْنٍ، عَنْ أَبِيهِ، أَنَّ رَسُولَ اللهِ ﷺ قَالَ: «**إِنَّ الْبَخِيلَ لَمَنْ ذُكِرْتُ عِنْدَهُ فَلَمْ يُصَلِّ عَلَيَّ**».

---

57 Al-Albānī said, "It is an authentic ḥadīth."

31. 'Ali b. Ḥusayn reported that his father reported that Allāh's Messenger ﷺ said, **"The stingy person is the one in whose presence I am mentioned but he does not send *ṣalāt* upon me."**[58]

٣٢ - حَدَّثَنَا يَحْيَىٰ بْنُ عَبْدِ الْحَمِيدِ، قَالَ: ثنا سُلَيْمَانُ بْنُ بِلَالٍ، عَنْ عُمَارَةَ بْنِ غَزِيَّةَ، عَنْ عَبْدِ اللهِ بْنِ عَلِيِّ بْنِ الْحُسَيْنِ، عَنْ أَبِيهِ، عَنْ جَدِّهِ قَالَ: قَالَ رَسُولُ اللهِ ﷺ: **«الْبَخِيلُ مَنْ ذُكِرْتُ عِنْدَهُ فَلَمْ يُصَلِّ عَلَيَّ»**. صَلَّىٰ اللهُ عَلَيْهِ وَسَلَّمَ تَسْلِيمًا.

32. 'Abdullāh b. 'Alī b. al-Ḥusayn reported that his father stated that his grandfather [al-Ḥusayn b. 'Alī b. Abī Ṭālib] reported that Allāh's Messenger ﷺ said, **"The stingy person is the one in whose presence I am mentioned but does not send *ṣalāt* upon me."**[59] *Ṣalla 'llāhu 'alayhi wa sallam taslīmā.*

قَالَ الْقَاضِي: اخْتَلَفَ يَحْيَىٰ الْحِمَّانِيُّ وَأَبُو بَكْرِ ابْنُ أَبِي أُوَيْسٍ فِي إِسْنَادِ هَذَا الْحَدِيثِ فَرَوَاهُ أَبُو بَكْرٍ عَنْ سُلَيْمَانَ عَنْ عَمْرِو ابْنِ أَبِي عَمْرٍو، وَرَوَاهُ الْحِمَّانِيُّ عَنْ سليمانَ بْنِ بِلَالٍ، عَنْ عُمَارَةَ بْنِ غَزِيَّةَ، وَهَذَا حَدِيثٌ مُشْتَهَرٌ عَنْ عُمَارَةَ بْنِ غَزِيَّةَ، وَرَوَاهُ عَنْهُ خَمْسَةٌ بَعْدَ سُلَيْمَانَ بْنِ بِلَالٍ وَعَمْرُو بْنُ الْحَارِثِ.

Al-Qāḍī said, "Yaḥyā al-Ḥimmāni and Abū Bakr b. Abī Uways dif-

58 [T] Reported by Aḥmad (1736) al-Tirmidhī (3546), and others. Al-Ḥākim judged it as authentic, and al-Albānī remarked that it has a great chain of narration.

59 Al-Albānī said, "This ḥadīth is authentic, just as the one before it."

fered in the chain of narration of this ḥadīth. Abū Bakr reported it from Sulaymān, who reported it from ʿAmr b. Abī ʿAmr, while al-Ḥimmāni reported it from Sulaymān b. Bilāl, who reported from ʿUmarah b. Ghaziyyah. This ḥadīth is famously narrated from ʿUmarah b. Ghaziyyah, and five other narrators reported it after Sulaymān b. Bilāl and ʿAmr b. al-Ḥārith.

٣٣ - فَحَدَّثَنَا بِهِ أَحْمَدُ بْنُ عِيسَى، قَالَ: ثنا عَبْدُ اللهِ بْنُ وَهْبٍ، أَخْبَرَنِي عَمْرٌو - وَهُوَ: ابْنُ الْحَارِثِ بْنِ يَعْقُوبَ - عَنْ عُمَارَةَ - يَعْنِي: ابْنَ غَزِيَّةَ، أَنَّ عَبْدَ اللهِ بْنَ عَلِيِّ بْنِ حُسَيْنٍ، حَدَّثَهُ أَنَّهُ سَمِعَ أَبَاهُ، يَقُولُ: قَالَ رَسُولُ اللهِ ﷺ: «إِنَّ الْبَخِيلَ مَنْ ذُكِرْتُ عِنْدَهُ فَلَمْ يُصَلِّ عَلَيَّ».

33. ʿAbdullāh b. ʿAlī b. al-Ḥusayn reported that he heard his father say, "Allāh's Messenger ﷺ said, **'The stingy person is the one in whose presence I am mentioned but does not send *ṣalāt* upon me.'**"[60]

قَالَ: هَكَذَا رَوَاهُ عَمْرُو بْنُ الْحَارِثِ أَرْسَلَهُ عَنْ عَلِيِّ بْنِ حُسَيْنٍ، عَنِ النَّبِيِّ ﷺ.

The author said: This is how ʿAmr b. al-Ḥārith reported it; he narrated it in *mursal* form from ʿAlī b. al-Ḥusayn, from the Prophet ﷺ.

60 [T] This narration is *mursal*, as Zayd al-Ābidīn, whose name was ʿAlī b. al-Ḥusayn b. ʿAlī b. Abī Ṭālib, was one of the Tābiʿīn, not one of the companions. However, as previously seen, there are many narrations similar to this one that are authentic, so this narration is also authentic, as al-Albānī also remarked.

٣٤ - قَالَ الْقَاضِي: وثنا بِهِ إِبْرَاهِيمُ بْنُ حَمْزَةَ، قَالَ: ثنا عَبْدُ الْعَزِيزِ - يَعْنِي: ابْنَ مُحَمَّدٍ الدَّرَاوَرْدِيَّ، عَنْ عُمَارَةَ - وَهُوَ: ابْنُ غَزِيَّةَ - عَنْ عَبْدِ اللهِ بْنِ حُسَيْنٍ، قَالَ: قَالَ عَلِيُّ ابْنُ أَبِي طَالِبٍ: قَالَ رَسُولُ اللهِ ﷺ: **«إِنَّ الْبَخِيلَ الَّذِي إِذَا ذُكِرْتُ عِنْدَهُ لَمْ يُصَلِّ عَلَيَّ»** ﷺ.

34. 'Alī b. Abī Ṭālib reported that Allāh's Messenger ﷺ said, **"The stingy person is the one in whose presence I am mentioned but does not send *ṣalāt* upon me."**[61]

هَكَذَا رَوَاهُ الدَّرَاوَرْدِيُّ، أَرْسَلَهُ عَنْ عَبْدِ اللهِ بْنِ عَلِيِّ بْنِ حُسَيْنٍ، عَنْ عَلِيٍّ رَضِيَ اللهُ عَنْهُ.

This was how it was reported by al-Darāwardī; he narrated it directly from 'Abdullāh b. 'Alī b. al-Ḥusayn, from 'Alī ﷺ.[62]

٣٥ - وَحَدَّثَنَا بِهِ إِسْحَاقُ بْنُ مُحَمَّدٍ الْفَرْوِيُّ، قَالَ: ثنا إِسْمَاعِيلُ بْنُ جَعْفَرٍ، عَنْ عُمَارَةَ بْنِ غَزِيَّةَ، أَنَّهُ سَمِعَ عَبْدَ اللهِ بْنَ عَلِيِّ بْنِ حُسَيْنٍ، يُحَدِّثُ عَنْ أَبِيهِ، عَنْ جَدِّهِ، أَنَّ رَسُولَ اللهِ ﷺ قَالَ: **«إِنَّ الْبَخِيلَ مَنْ ذُكِرْتُ عِنْدَهُ فَلَمْ يُصَلِّ عَلَيَّ»** ﷺ.

35. 'Abdullāh b. 'Alī b. Ḥusayn reported that his father said that his

61 Al-Albānī remarked, "The narrators are all trustworthy, but this chain of narration is missing some narrators." [T] The wording of the narration is also authentic, due to the many authentic narrations with the same wording.

62 [T] Meaning, he omitted 'Alī b. al-Ḥusayn as well as his father, al-Ḥusayn, and narrated it directly from 'Alī ﷺ. However, as previously mentioned, it does not harm the authenticity of the narration.

grandfather reported that Allāh's Messenger ﷺ said, **"The stingy person is the one in whose presence I am mentioned but he does not send *ṣalāt* upon me."**[63]

٣٦ - حَدَّثَنَا بِهِ عَلِيُّ بْنُ عَبْدِ اللهِ بْنِ جَعْفَرِ بْنِ نَجِيحٍ قَالَ: قَالَ أَبِي: ثنا عُمَارَةُ بْنُ غَزِيَّةَ، أَنَّهُ سَمِعَ عَبْدَ اللهِ بْنَ عَلِيِّ بْنِ حُسَيْنٍ، يُحَدِّثُ عَنْ أَبِيهِ، عَنْ جَدِّهِ، عَنْ رَسُولِ اللهِ ﷺ بِمِثْلِهِ.

36. A similar narration was narrated through another chain of narration from 'Abdullāh b. 'Alī b. Ḥusayn.

قَالَ الْقَاضِي: وَصَلَ عَبْدُ اللهِ بْنُ جَعْفَرٍ إِسْنَادَهُ، كَمَا ثنا بِهِ الْفَرْوِيُّ، عَنْ إِسْمَاعِيلَ بْنِ جَعْفَرٍ، وَكَمَا ثنا بِهِ الْحِمَّانِيُّ، عَنْ سُلَيْمَانَ بْنِ بِلَالٍ.

Al-Qāḍī said: 'Abdullāh b. Ja'far reported with a connected chain of narration, as narrated to us by al-Farawī, from Ismā'īl b. Ja'far, and as we were informed by al-Hammānī, who reported from Sulaymān b. Bilāl.

٣٧ - حَدَّثَنَا حَجَّاجُ بْنُ الْمِنْهَالِ قَالَ: ثنا حَمَّادُ بْنُ سَلَمَةَ، عَنْ مَعْبَدِ بْنِ هِلَالٍ الْعَنَزِيِّ قَالَ: حَدَّثَنِي رَجُلٌ مِنْ أَهْلِ دِمَشْقَ، عَنْ عَوْفِ بْنِ مَالِكٍ، عَنْ أَبِي ذَرٍّ، أَنَّ رَسُولَ اللهِ ﷺ قَالَ: **«إِنَّ أَبْخَلَ النَّاسِ مَنْ ذُكِرْتُ عِنْدَهُ فَلَمْ يُصَلِّ عَلَيَّ»** ﷺ.

37. Abū Dharr ؓ reported that Allāh's Messenger ﷺ said, **"The**

63 Al-Albānī said, "This has an authentic chain of narration up until 'Abdullāh b. 'Alī b. al-Ḥusayn."

stingiest of all people is the one in whose presence I am mentioned but he does not send *ṣalāt* upon me."[64]

٣٨ - حَدَّثَنَا سُلَيْمَانُ بْنُ حَرْبٍ، قَالَ: ثنا جَرِيرُ بْنُ حَازِمٍ، قَالَ: سَمِعْتُ الْحَسَنَ، يَقُولُ: قَالَ رَسُولُ اللهِ ﷺ: «**بِحَسْبِ امْرِئٍ فِي الْبُخْلِ أَنْ أُذْكَرَ عِنْدَهُ فَلَا يُصَلِّي عَلَيَّ**».

38. Al-Ḥasan said, "Allāh's Messenger ﷺ said, **'It is sufficient for a person to be stingy if I am mentioned in their presence but they do not send *ṣalāt* upon me.'"**[65]

٣٩ - حَدَّثَنَا سَلْمُ بْنُ سُلَيْمَانَ الضَّبِّيُّ، قَالَ: ثنا أَبُو حُرَّةَ، عَنِ الْحَسَنِ، قَالَ: قَالَ رَسُولُ اللهِ ﷺ: «**كَفَىٰ بِهِ شُحًّا أَنْ يَذْكُرَنِي قَوْمٌ فَلَا يُصَلُّونَ عَلَيَّ**» ﷺ.

39. Al-Ḥasan said that Allāh's Messenger ﷺ said, **"It is sufficient for a person to be miserly that people mention me but they do not send *ṣalāt* upon me."**[66]

---

64 Al-Albānī said, "This is an authentic narration, and is corroborated by the narration before it. It was also reported by Ibn Abī 'Āṣim in *Kitāb al-Ṣalāt* through another chain of narration, and both of these chains of narration support one another."

65 Al-Albānī remarked, "Though this chain of narration is *mursal*, it is authentic [up to al-Ḥasan al-Baṣrī] and is strengthened by the supporting narrations before it."

66 Al-Albānī said, "The chain of narration is *mursal* and weak, but it is corroborated by the previous narrations."

٤٠ - حَدَّثَنَا عَارِمٌ قَالَ: ثنا جَرِيرُ بْنُ حَازِمٍ، عَنِ الْحَسَنِ، قَالَ: قَالَ رَسُولُ اللهِ ﷺ: «أَكْثِرُوا عَلَيَّ مِنَ الصَّلَاةِ يَوْمَ الْجُمُعَةِ».

40. Al-Ḥasan said that Allāh's Messenger ﷺ said, **"Send abundant *ṣalāt* upon me on Fridays."**[67]

٤١ - حَدَّثَنَا إِسْمَاعِيلُ بْنُ أَبِي أُوَيْسٍ، قَالَ: ثنا سُلَيْمَانُ بْنُ بِلَالٍ، عَنْ جَعْفَرٍ، عَنْ أَبِيهِ، أَنَّ النَّبِيَّ ﷺ قَالَ: «مَنْ نَسِيَ الصَّلَاةَ عَلَيَّ خَطِئَ أَبْوَابَ الْجَنَّةِ».

41. Jaʿfar reported from his father [Muḥammad b. ʿAlī b. al-Ḥusayn b. ʿAlī b. Abī Ṭālib] that the Prophet ﷺ said, **"Whoever forgets to send *ṣalāt* upon me will be made to miss the doors of paradise."**[68]

٤٢ - حَدَّثَنَا عَلِيُّ بْنُ عَبْدِ اللهِ قَالَ: ثنا سُفْيَانُ قَالَ: قَالَ عَمْرٌو، عَنْ مُحَمَّدِ بْنِ عَلِيِّ بْنِ حُسَيْنٍ، قَالَ: قَالَ رَسُولُ اللهِ ﷺ: «مَنْ يَنْسَى الصَّلَاةَ عَلَيَّ خَطِئَ طَرِيقَ الْجَنَّةِ».

---

67 Al-Albānī said, "This chain of narration is *mursal* but the wording is corroborated by ḥadīth 22 in this very book."

68 [T] This ḥadīth is *mursal*. [T] Al-Albānī mentioned that it was also reported with a complete chain of narration by al-Ṭabarānī. It was reported by Ibn Mājah through a different, though weak, chain of narration (908). Ibn Shāhīn also reported it (81) through his own chain of narration through Abū Hurayrah ؓ, but commented, "It was singularly reported by ʿUmar b. Ḥafṣ from his father; I am not aware that anyone else reported this particular narration from Ḥafṣ." His chain of narration is *ḥasan*. Therefore, when accounting for all of the corroborating narrations, this ḥadīth is *ḥasan* at worst.

42. Muḥammad b. 'Alī b. al-Ḥusayn said that Allāh's Messenger ﷺ said, **"Whoever forgets to send *ṣalāt* upon me will be made to miss the path of paradise."**

قَالَ سُفْيَانُ: قَالَ رَجُلٌ بَعْدَ عَمْرٍو: سَمِعْتُ مُحَمَّدَ بْنَ عَلِيٍّ يَقُولُ: قَالَ رَسُولُ اللهِ ﷺ: **«مَنْ ذُكِرْتُ عِنْدَهُ فَلَمْ يُصَلِّ عَلَيَّ خَطِئَ طَرِيقَ الْجَنَّةِ»**.

Sufyān said, "After 'Amr, there was another man mentioned. I heard Muḥammad b. 'Alī say that Allāh's Messenger ﷺ said, **'Whoever does not send *ṣalāt* upon me when I am mentioned in their presence will be made to miss the path of paradise.'**"

ثُمَّ سَمَّىٰ سُفْيَانُ الرَّجُلَ فَقَالَ: هُوَ: بَسَّامٌ - وَهُوَ: الصَّيْرَفِيُّ.

Then, Sufyān named the man as "Bassām al-Ṣayrafī."[69]

٤٣ - حَدَّثَنَا سُلَيْمَانُ بْنُ حَرْبٍ، وَعَارِمٌ قَالَ: ثنا حَمَّادُ بْنُ زَيْدٍ، عَنْ عَمْرٍو، عَنْ مُحَمَّدِ بْنِ عَلِيٍّ قَالَ: قَالَ رَسُولُ اللهِ ﷺ: **«مَنْ نَسِيَ الصَّلَاةَ عَلَيَّ خَطِئَ طَرِيقَ الْجَنَّةِ»**.

43. Muḥammad b. 'Alī said that Allāh's Messenger ﷺ said, **"Whoever forgets to send *ṣalāt* upon me will be made to miss the path of paradise."**[70]

٤٤ - حَدَّثَنَا إِبْرَاهِيمُ بْنُ حَجَّاجٍ قَالَ: ثنا وُهَيْبٌ، عَنْ جَعْفَرِ بْنِ مُحَمَّدٍ، عَنْ أَبِيهِ، أَنَّ النَّبِيَّ ﷺ قَالَ: **«مَنْ ذُكِرْتُ عِنْدَهُ فَلَمْ يُصَلِّ عَلَيَّ فَقَدْ خَطِئَ**

69 Al-Albānī said, "It is authentic, though *mursal*."
70 Al-Albānī said, "It is authentic, though *mursal*."

طَرِيقَ الْجَنَّةِ».

44. Jaʿfar b. Muḥammad reported that his father [Muḥammad b. ʿAlī] reported that the Prophet ﷺ said, **"When I am mentioned in the presence of someone and they do not send ṣalāt upon me, they have missed the path of paradise."**[71]

٤٥ - حَدَّثَنَا مُحَمَّدُ بْنُ أَبِي بَكْرٍ الْمُقَدَّمِيُّ، قَالَ: ثنا عُمَرُ بْنُ هَارُونَ، عَنْ مُوسَىٰ بْنِ عُبَيْدَةَ، عَنْ مُحَمَّدِ بْنِ ثَابِتٍ، عَنْ أَبِي هُرَيْرَةَ، أَنَّ النَّبِيَّ ﷺ قَالَ: «صَلُّوا عَلَىٰ أَنْبِيَاءِ اللهِ وَرُسُلِهِ؛ فَإِنَّ اللهَ بَعَثَهُمْ كَمَا بَعَثَنِي». صَلَّىٰ اللهُ عَلَيْهِ وَسَلَّمَ وَعَلَيْهِمُ السَّلَامُ.

45. Abū Hurayrah ؓ reported that the Prophet ﷺ said, **"Send ṣalāt upon the prophets and messengers of Allāh, for He has sent them just as He has sent me."**[72] May Allāh send his peace and blessings upon him and send salutations upon them.

٤٦ - حَدَّثَنَا سُلَيْمَانُ بْنُ حَرْبٍ، قَالَ: ثنا سَعِيدُ بْنُ زَيْدٍ، عَنْ لَيْثٍ، عَنْ كَعْبٍ، عَنْ أَبِي هُرَيْرَةَ قَالَ: قَالَ رَسُولُ اللهِ ﷺ: «صَلُّوا عَلَيَّ فَإِنَّ صَلَاتَكُمْ عَلَيَّ زَكَاةٌ لَكُمْ» قَالَ: «وَسَلُوا اللهَ لِيَ الْوَسِيلَةَ» قَالَ: فَإِمَّا حَدَّثَنَا وَإِمَّا سَأَلْنَاهُ؟ - قَالَ ﷺ: «الْوَسِيلَةُ: أَعْلَىٰ دَرَجَةٍ فِي الْجَنَّةِ، لَا يَنَالُهَا إِلَّا رَجُلٌ وَأَرْجُو أَنْ أَكُونَ أَنَا ذَلِكَ الرَّجُلَ».

---

71 Al-Albānī said, "It is authentic, though *mursal*." [T] As mentioned, all of these wordings serve the same meaning, and the meaning is authentic.

72 Al-Albānī remarked that this chain of narration is very weak.

46. Abū Hurayrah ؓ said that Allāh's Messenger ﷺ said, **"Send *ṣalāt* upon me, for your *ṣalāt* upon me is a means of purification for you. And ask Allāh to grant me *al-wasīlah*."** Abū Hurayrah ؓ said, "He either told us what it meant on his own, or we asked him what it meant, and he said, **'*Al-wasīlah* is the highest rank in paradise. Only one man shall receive it, and I hope to be that man.'"**[73]

٤٧ - حَدَّثَنَا مُحَمَّدُ بْنُ أَبِي بَكْرٍ قَالَ: ثنا مُعْتَمِرٌ، عَنْ لَيْثٍ، عَنْ كَعْبٍ، عَنِ النَّبِيِّ ﷺ قَالَ: «**صَلُّوا عَلَيَّ فَإِنَّ صَلَاتَكُمْ عَلَيَّ زَكَاةٌ لَكُمْ، وَسَلُوا اللهَ لِيَ الْوَسِيلَةَ**» - فَإِمَّا أَنْ يَكُونُوا سَأَلُوهُ، وَإِمَّا أَنْ يَكُونَ أَخْبَرَهُمْ - قَالَ: «**إِنَّهَا أَعْلَىٰ دَرَجَةٍ فِي الْجَنَّةِ لَا يَنَالُهَا إِلَّا رَجُلٌ وَاحِدٌ وَأَرْجُو أَنْ أَكُونَ أَنَا هُوَ**».

47. Ka'b reported that the Prophet ﷺ said, **"Send *ṣalāt* upon me, for your *ṣalāt* upon me are a means of purification for you. And ask Allāh to grant me *al-wasīlah*."** [Ka'b said] "They either asked him [what *al-wasīlah* is] or he told them on his own, but he said, **'It is the highest rank in paradise. Only one man shall receive it, and I hope to be that man.'"**[74]

٤٨ - حَدَّثَنَا مُحَمَّدُ بْنُ أَبِي بَكْرٍ، قَالَ: ثنا الضَّحَّاكُ بْنُ مَخْلَدٍ، قَالَ: ثنا مُوسَىٰ بْنُ عُبَيْدَةَ، أَخْبَرَنِي مُحَمَّدُ بْنُ عَمْرِو بْنِ عَطَاءٍ، عَنِ ابْنِ عَبَّاسٍ قَالَ: قَالَ رَسُولُ اللهِ ﷺ: «**سَلُوا اللهَ لِيَ الْوَسِيلَةَ؛ لَا يَسْأَلُهَا لِي مُسْلِمٌ أَوْ مُؤْمِنٌ**

73 Al-Albānī stated that it has a weak chain of narration. However, the last part of the ḥadīth is authentic, and it has corroborating narrations elsewhere, such as in this very book, under ḥadīth 50.

74 Al-Albānī said this is weak.

إِلَّا كُنْتُ لَهُ شَهِيدًا أَوْ شَفِيعًا أَوْ شَفِيعًا أَوْ شَهِيدًا».

48. Ibn 'Abbās said that Allāh's Messenger ﷺ said, **"Ask Allāh to grant me *al-wasīlah*, for whenever a Muslim or believer asks for it for me, I will be a witness or an intercessor for them (or, an intercessor or a witness)."**[75]

٤٩ - حَدَّثَنَا إِسْحَاقُ بْنُ مُحَمَّدٍ الْفَرْوِيُّ قَالَ: ثنا إِسْمَاعِيلُ بْنُ جَعْفَرٍ، عَنْ عُمَارَةَ - وَهُوَ: ابْنُ غَزِيَّةَ - عَنْ مُوسَىٰ بْنِ وَرْدَانَ، أَنَّهُ سَمِعَ أَبَا سَعِيدٍ الْخُدْرِيَّ، يَقُولُ: قَالَ رَسُولُ اللهِ ﷺ: «إِنَّ الْوَسِيلَةَ دَرَجَةٌ عِنْدَ اللهِ لَيْسَ فَوْقَهَا دَرَجَةٌ، فَسَلُوا اللهَ أَنْ يُؤْتِيَنِي الْوَسِيلَةَ عَلَىٰ خَلْقِهِ».

49. Abū Sa'īd al-Khudrī reported that Allāh's Messenger ﷺ said, **"*Al-wasīlah* is a rank with Allāh above which there are no ranks. Ask Allāh to grant me *al-wasīlah* over all of his creation."**[76]

٥٠ - حَدَّثَنَا مُحَمَّدُ بْنُ أَبِي بَكْرٍ قَالَ: ثنا عُمَرُ بْنُ عَلِيٍّ، عَنْ أَبِي بَكْرٍ الْجُشَمِيِّ، عَنْ صَفْوَانَ بْنِ سُلَيْمٍ، عَنْ عَبْدِ اللهِ بْنِ عَمْرٍو قَالَ: قَالَ رَسُولُ اللهِ ﷺ «مَنْ صَلَّىٰ عَلَيَّ أَوْ سَأَلَ لِيَ الْوَسِيلَةَ، حَقَّتْ عَلَيْهِ شَفَاعَتِي يَوْمَ الْقِيَامَةِ».

50. 'Abdullāh b. 'Amr said that Allāh's Messenger ﷺ said, **"Whoev-**

---

75 Al-Albānī mentioned that the chain of narration is weak, but the meaning could be considered authentic as it has corroborating evidences. [T] It was also reported by al-Tirmidhī (3612) through largely the same narrators.
76 Al-Albānī said the chain of narration is *ḥasan*.

er sends *ṣalāt* upon me, or asks Allāh to grant me *al-wasīlah*, will earn the right of my intercession on the Day of Resurrection."[77]

٥١ - حَدَّثَنَا مُحَمَّدٌ قَالَ: ثنا عَبْدُ اللهِ بْنُ جَعْفَرٍ، أَخْبَرَنِي عَبْدُ الرَّحْمَنِ بْنُ مُحَمَّدِ بْنِ عَبْدٍ الْقَارِيُّ، عَنْ عَوْنِ بْنِ عَبْدِ اللهِ، أَنَّ النَّبِيَّ ﷺ قَالَ: «إِنَّ فِي الْجَنَّةِ مَجْلِسًا لَمْ يُعْطَهُ أَحَدٌ قَبْلِي، وَأَنَا أَرْجُو أَنْ أُعْطَاهُ؛ فَسَلُوا اللهَ لِيَ الْوَسِيلَةَ».

51. 'Awn b. 'Abdillāh reported that the Prophet ﷺ said, **"In paradise, there is a seat that has never been given to a person before me, and I hope to be given it, so ask Allāh to grant me *al-wasīlah*."**[78]

٥٢ - حَدَّثَنَا عَلِيُّ بْنُ عَبْدِ اللهِ، قَالَ: ثنا سُفْيَانُ، حَدَّثَنِي مَعْمَرٌ، عَنْ عَبْدِ اللهِ بْنِ طَاوُسٍ، عَنْ أَبِيهِ، قَالَ: سَمِعْتُ ابْنَ عَبَّاسٍ يَقُولُ: اللَّهُمَّ تَقَبَّلْ شَفَاعَةَ مُحَمَّدٍ الْكُبْرَىٰ، وَارْفَعْ دَرَجَتَهُ الْعُلْيَا وَأَعْطِهِ سُؤْلَهُ فِي الْآخِرَةِ وَالْأُولَىٰ كَمَا آتَيْتَ إِبْرَاهِيمَ وَمُوسَىٰ عَلَيْهِمُ السَّلَامُ.

52. Ibn 'Abbās said, "Allāh, accept the major intercession of Muḥammad, raise his rank high, and grant his wishes in the hereafter and the worldly life, as you gave those privileges to Ibrāhīm and Mūsā ﷺ."[79]

77 Al-Albānī said it is an authentic ḥadīth, and is corroborated by a ḥadīth in the *Ṣaḥīḥ* of Imām Muslim (384).

78 Al-Albānī remarked that the chain of narration is weak, but the meaning is testified to by other similar narrations.

79 [T] Reported by 'Abd al-Razzāq (3104) with a chain of narration that

٥٣ - حَدَّثَنَا يَحْيَىٰ قَالَ: ثنا زَيْدُ بْنُ حُبَابٍ، أَخْبَرَنِي ابْنُ لَهِيعَةَ، حَدَّثَنِي بَكْرُ بْنُ سَوَادَةَ الْمَعَافِرِيُّ، عَنْ زِيَادِ بْنِ نُعَيْمٍ الْحَضْرَمِيِّ، عَنِ ابْنِ شُرَيْحٍ قَالَ: حَدَّثَنِي رُوَيْفِعٌ الْأَنْصَارِيُّ، أَنَّهُ سَمِعَ النَّبِيَّ ﷺ يَقُولُ: **«مَنْ قَالَ: اللَّهُمَّ صَلِّ عَلَىٰ مُحَمَّدٍ وَأَنْزِلْهُ الْمَقْعَدَ الْمُقَرَّبَ مِنْكَ يَوْمَ الْقِيَامَةِ، وَجَبَتْ لَهُ الشَّفَاعَةُ»**.

53. Ruwayfiʿ al-Anṣārī stated that he heard the Prophet ﷺ say, **"Whoever says, 'Allāh, send *ṣalāt* upon Muḥammad and allow him to sit in the seating that is close to You on the Day of Resurrection *(Allāhumma ṣalli 'alā Muḥammad, wa anzilhu 'l-maq'ada 'l-muqarraba minka yawma 'l-qiyāmah),'* will be owed intercession."**[80]

٥٤ - حَدَّثَنَا مُحَمَّدُ بْنُ كَثِيرٍ، قَالَ: ثنا سُفْيَانُ بْنُ سَعِيدٍ، عَنْ صَالِحٍ مَوْلَىٰ التَّوْأَمَةِ عَنْ أَبِي هُرَيْرَةَ قَالَ: قَالَ رَسُولُ اللهِ ﷺ: **«مَا جَلَسَ قَوْمٌ مَجْلِسًا لَمْ يَذْكُرُوا اللهَ، وَلَمْ يُصَلُّوا عَلَىٰ نَبِيِّهِمْ ﷺ، إِلَّا كَانَ مَجْلِسُهُمْ عَلَيْهِمْ تِرَةً يَوْمَ الْقِيَامَةِ إِنْ شَاءَ عَفَا عَنْهُمْ، وَإِنْ شَاءَ أَخَذَهُمْ»**.

54. Abū Hurayrah رضي الله عنه said that Allāh's Messenger ﷺ said, **"There are no people who sit in a gathering wherein they do not mention Allāh and do not send *ṣalāt* upon their prophet ﷺ, except that their gathering is a source of regret for them on the Day**

---

was judged as authentic by al-Albānī and before him, Ibn Kathīr in his *Tafsīr* (6/461).

80 Al-Albānī remarked that this chain of narration is weak due to the presence of Ibn Lahī'ah. Al-Haythamī judged it as *ḥasan*.

of Resurrection. If Allāh so wishes, He shall forgive them, and if He so wishes, He shall seize them."[81]

٥٥ - حَدَّثَنَا عَاصِمُ بْنُ عَلِيٍّ، وَحَفْصُ بْنُ عُمَرَ، وَسُلَيْمَانُ بْنُ حَرْبٍ، قَالُوا: ثنا شُعْبَةُ، عَنْ سُلَيْمَانَ، عَنْ ذَكْوَانَ، عَنْ أَبِي سَعِيدٍ قَالَ: مَا مِنْ قَوْمٍ يَقْعُدُونَ ثُمَّ يَقُومُونَ وَلَا يُصَلُّونَ عَلَى النَّبِيِّ ﷺ إِلَّا كَانَ عَلَيْهِمْ يَوْمَ الْقِيَامَةِ حَسْرَةً، وَإِنْ دَخَلُوا الْجَنَّةَ لِلثَّوَابِ.

55. Abū Sa'īd said, "There are no people that gather and then arise from their gathering without sending *ṣalāt* upon the Prophet ﷺ except that it is a regret for them on the Day of Resurrection, even if they enter paradise, for they will see their lost [opportunities of] rewards."[82]

وَهَذَا لَفْظُ الْحَوْضِيِّ.

This is the wording of al-Ḥawḍī.

٥٦ - حَدَّثَنَا سُلَيْمَانُ، قَالَ: ثنا شُعْبَةُ، عَنِ الْحَكَمِ، عَنِ ابْنِ أَبِي لَيْلَىٰ، عَنْ كَعْبِ بْنِ عُجْرَةَ، أَنَّهُ قَالَ: أَلَا أُهْدِي لَكَ هَدِيَّةً؟ إِنَّ رَسُولَ اللهِ ﷺ خَرَجَ

---

81 [T] Reported by Aḥmad (10277) and al-Tirmidhī. Al-Albānī remarked that it is an authentic chain of narration.

82 Al-Albānī said, "The chain of narration is authentic, and it has the ruling of a ḥadīth directly attributed to the Prophet ﷺ, especially since it has been reported directly to the Prophet ﷺ and was reported by Aḥmad [9965]." The ḥadīth directly attributed to the Prophet ﷺ was also reported by al-Nasā'ī in *al-Kubrā* (10242) and al-Bayhaqī in *Shu'ab al-Īmān* (1470).

عَلَيْنَا، قَالَ: فَقُلْنَا يَا رَسُولَ اللهِ قَدْ عَلِمْنَا كَيْفَ نُسَلِّمُ عَلَيْكَ، فَكَيْفَ نُصَلِّي؟ قَالَ: «قُولُوا: اللَّهُمَّ صَلِّ عَلَىٰ مُحَمَّدٍ وَعَلَىٰ آلِ مُحَمَّدٍ كَمَا صَلَّيْتَ عَلَىٰ آلِ إِبْرَاهِيمَ إِنَّكَ حَمِيدٌ مَجِيدٌ».

56. Ka'b b. 'Ujrah ﷺ said, "Shall I not give you a gift? Allāh's Messenger ﷺ once entered our presence and we said to him, 'Messenger of Allāh, we know how to salute you, but how do we send *ṣalāt* upon you?' He replied, **'Say: Allāh, send *ṣalāt* upon Muḥammad and upon the family of Muḥammad, as you have sent *ṣalāt* upon the family of Ibrāhīm, truly, you are Praiseworthy and Glorious *(Allāhumma ṣalli 'ala Muḥammadin wa 'alā Āli Muḥammad, kamā ṣallayta 'alā Āli Ibrāhīm, innaka Ḥamīdu 'm-Majīd).'*"**[83]

٥٧ - حَدَّثَنَا مُسَدَّدٌ، قَالَ: ثنا هُشَيْمٌ، عَنْ يَزِيدَ بْنِ أَبِي زِيَادٍ، عَنْ عَبْدِ الرَّحْمَنِ بْنِ أَبِي لَيْلَىٰ، عَنْ كَعْبِ بْنِ عُجْرَةَ، قَالَ: لَمَّا نَزَلَتْ هَذِهِ الْآيَةُ ﴿إِنَّ اللهَ وَمَلَائِكَتَهُ يُصَلُّونَ عَلَى النَّبِيِّ يَا أَيُّهَا الَّذِينَ آمَنُوا صَلُّوا عَلَيْهِ وَسَلِّمُوا تَسْلِيمًا﴾ [الأحزاب: ٥٦] قُلْنَا: يَا رَسُولَ اللهِ قَدْ عَلِمْنَا السَّلَامَ عَلَيْكَ فَكَيْفَ الصَّلَاةُ عَلَيْكَ؟ قَالَ: «تَقُولُونَ: اللَّهُمَّ صَلِّ عَلَىٰ مُحَمَّدٍ وَعَلَىٰ آلِ مُحَمَّدٍ كَمَا صَلَّيْتَ عَلَىٰ إِبْرَاهِيمَ وَآلِ إِبْرَاهِيمَ، إِنَّكَ حَمِيدٌ مَجِيدٌ وَبَارِكْ عَلَىٰ مُحَمَّدٍ وَعَلَىٰ آلِ مُحَمَّدٍ كَمَا بَارَكْتَ وَصَلَّيْتَ عَلَىٰ إِبْرَاهِيمَ وَآلِ إِبْرَاهِيمَ، إِنَّكَ حَمِيدٌ مَجِيدٌ».

---

83 Al-Albānī remarked that the chain of narration is authentic. [T] This version of the *ṣalāt* was reported by 'Abd al-Razzāq in *al-Muṣannaf* (3106).

57. Ka'b b. 'Ujrah ﷺ reported, "When Allāh revealed the following verse: **{Surely, Allāh and His angels send *ṣalāt* upon the Prophet. O you who believe, send *ṣalāt* upon him, and send salutations to him in abundance.}** [Qur'ān 33:56] We said, 'Messenger of Allāh, we know how to salute you, but how is the *ṣalāt* upon you [uttered]?' He replied, **'By saying: Allāh, send *ṣalāt* upon Muḥammad and upon the family of Muḥammad, as you have sent *ṣalāt* upon Ibrāhīm and upon the family of Ibrāhīm, truly, you are Praiseworthy and Glorious. And send blessings upon Muḥammad and upon the family of Muḥammad, as you have sent blessings and salutations upon Ibrāhīm and upon the family of Ibrāhīm, truly, you are Praiseworthy and Glorious *(Allāhumma ṣalli 'ala Muḥammadin wa 'alā Āli Muḥammad, kamā ṣallayta 'alā Ibrāhīm, wa 'alā Āli Ibrāhīm innaka Ḥamīdu 'm-Majīd, wa bārik 'ala Muḥammadin wa 'alā Āli Muḥammad, kamā bārakta wa ṣallayta 'alā Ibrāhīm, wa 'alā Āli Ibrāhīm, innaka Ḥamīdu 'm-Majīd).*'"**[84]

قَالَ: وَكَانَ ابْنُ أَبِي لَيْلَىٰ يَقُولُ: وَعَلَيْنَا مَعَهُمْ.

Ibn Abī Laylā would add, "And upon us with them."

٥٨ - حَدَّثَنَا مُسَدَّدٌ، قَالَ: ثنا أَبُو الْأَحْوَصِ، قَالَ: ثنا يَزِيدُ بْنُ أَبِي زِيَادٍ، عَنْ عَبْدِ الرَّحْمَنِ بْنِ أَبِي لَيْلَىٰ، عَنْ كَعْبِ بْنِ عُجْرَةَ قَالَ: قُلْتُ: يَا رَسُولَ اللهِ قَدْ عَرَفْنَا السَّلَامَ عَلَيْكَ، فَكَيْفَ الصَّلَاةُ عَلَيْكَ؟ قَالَ: «تَقُولُونَ: اللَّهُمَّ

84 Al-Albānī remarked, "The chain of narration is weak." [T] It was reported by 'Abd al-Razzāq in *al-Muṣannaf* (3107) with an authentic chain of narration.

صَلِّ عَلَىٰ مُحَمَّدٍ وَعَلَىٰ آلِ مُحَمَّدٍ، كَمَا صَلَّيْتَ عَلَىٰ إِبْرَاهِيمَ، وَآلِ إِبْرَاهِيمَ إِنَّكَ حَمِيدٌ مَجِيدٌ». قَالَ: وَنَحْنُ نَقُولُ: وَعَلَيْنَا مَعَهُمْ.

58. Ka'b b. 'Ujrah ﷺ said, "I said, 'Messenger of Allāh, we know how to salute you, but how do we send the *ṣalāt* upon you?' He replied, **'It is by saying: Allāh, send *ṣalāt* upon Muḥammad and upon the family of Muḥammad, as you have sent *ṣalāt* upon Ibrāhīm and the family of Ibrāhīm, truly, you are Praiseworthy and Glorious *(Allāhumma ṣalli 'ala Muḥammadin wa 'alā Āli Muḥammad, kamā ṣallayta 'alā Ibrāhīm, wa Āli Ibrāhīm innaka Ḥamīdu 'm-Majīd).*'"**[85] He said, "And we say, 'And upon us with them.'"

٥٩ - حَدَّثَنَا أَحْمَدُ بْنُ عَبْدِ اللهِ بْنِ يُونُسَ، قَالَ: ثنا زُهَيْرٌ قَالَ: ثنا مُحَمَّدُ بْنُ إِسْحَاقَ، قَالَ: ثنا مُحَمَّدُ بْنُ إِبْرَاهِيمَ بْنِ الْحَارِثِ، عَنْ مُحَمَّدِ بْنِ عَبْدِ اللهِ بْنِ زَيدٍ، عَنْ عُقْبَةَ بْنِ عَمْرٍو، قَالَ: أَتَىٰ رَسُولَ اللهِ رَجُلٌ حَتَّىٰ جَلَسَ بَيْنَ يَدَيْهِ، فَقَالَ: يَا رَسُولَ اللهِ أَمَّا السَّلَامُ عَلَيْكَ فَقَدْ عَرَفْنَاهُ، وَأَمَا الصَّلَاةُ فَأَخْبِرْنَا بِهَا، كَيْفَ نُصَلِّي عَلَيْكَ؟ قَالَ: فَصَمَتَ رَسُولُ اللهِ ﷺ حَتَّىٰ وَدِدْنَا أَنَّ الرَّجُلَ الَّذِي سَأَلَهُ لَمْ يَسْأَلْهُ.

59. 'Uqbah b. 'Amr said, "A man approached Allāh's Messenger ﷺ,

---

85 [T] This chain of narration is also weak, as it is the same as the previous narration, which is that it contains Ibn Abī Laylā who was declared weak, as al-Albānī remarked. However, when taking all of the wordings of this narration into account, the ḥadīth is authentic. It should be noted that Ibn Abī Laylā is one of the narrators deemed worthy by Muslim in his *Ṣaḥīḥ*, and he reported wordings of this ḥadīth (406).

sat before him and said, 'Messenger of Allāh, as for saluting you, we know how to do that, but as for *ṣalāt* upon you, tell us how to send *ṣalāt* upon you.' Allāh's Messenger ﷺ remained silent until we wished that the man had not asked him the question.

ثُمَّ قَالَ: «إِذَا صَلَّيْتُمْ عَلَيَّ فَقُولُوا: اللَّهُمَّ صَلِّ عَلَىٰ مُحَمَّدٍ النَّبِيِّ الْأُمِّيِّ، وَعَلَىٰ آلِ مُحَمَّدٍ كَمَا صَلَّيْتَ عَلَىٰ إِبْرَاهِيمَ، وَعَلَىٰ آلِ إِبْرَاهِيمَ وَبَارِكْ عَلَىٰ مُحَمَّدٍ النَّبِيِّ الْأُمِّيِّ، وَعَلَىٰ آلِ مُحَمَّدٍ، كَمَا بَارَكْتَ عَلَىٰ إِبْرَاهِيمَ وَعَلَىٰ آلِ إِبْرَاهِيمَ إِنَّكَ حَمِيدٌ مَجِيدٌ».

Then, he said, **'If you were to send *ṣalāt* upon me, say: Allāh, send *ṣalāt* upon Muḥammad, the unlettered prophet, and upon the family of Muḥammad, as you have sent *ṣalāt* upon Ibrāhīm and upon the family of Ibrāhīm. Also, send blessings upon Muḥammad, the unlettered prophet, and upon the family of Muḥammad, as you have sent blessings upon Ibrāhīm and the family of Ibrāhīm. Truly, you are Praiseworthy and Glorious *(Allāhumma ṣalli 'ala Muḥammadin 'n-Nabiyyi 'l-Ummi wa 'alā Āli Muḥammad kamā ṣallayta 'alā Ibrāhīm, wa Āli Ibrāhīm. Wa bārik 'ala Muḥammadin 'n-Nabiyyi 'l-Ummi wa 'alā Āli Muḥammad, kamā bārakta 'alā Ibrāhīm, wa 'alā Āli Ibrāhīm. Innaka Ḥamīdu 'm-Majīd).*'"**[86]

٦٠ - حَدَّثَنَا سُلَيْمَانُ بْنُ حَرْبٍ قَالَ: ثنا حَمَّادُ بْنُ سَلَمَةَ قَالَ: ثنا سَعِيدٌ الْجُرَيْرِيُّ، عَنْ يَزِيد بْنِ عَبْدِ اللهِ، أَنَّهُمْ كَانُوا يَسْتَحِبُّونَ أَنْ يَقُولُوا: اللَّهُمَّ

86 Al-Albānī remarked, "The chain of narration is *ḥasan*." It was also reported by Aḥmad (17072) and Ibn Khuzaymah (711).

صَلِّ عَلَىٰ مُحَمَّدٍ النَّبِيِّ الْأُمِّيِّ، عَلَيْهِ السَّلَامُ.

60. Yazīd b. ʿAbdillāh reported that they would find it recommended to say, "Allāh, send *ṣalāt* upon Muḥammad, the unlettered prophet ﷺ."[87]

٦١ – حَدَّثَنَا عَاصِمُ بْنُ عَلِيٍّ قَالَ: ثنا الْمَسْعُودِيُّ، عَنْ عَوْنِ بْنِ عَبْدِ اللهِ، عَنْ أَبِي فَاخِتَةَ، عَنِ الْأَسْوَدِ، عَنْ عَبْدِ اللهِ، أَنَّهُ قَالَ: إِذَا صَلَّيْتُمْ عَلَىٰ النَّبِيِّ ﷺ فَأَحْسِنُوا الصَّلَاةَ عَلَيْهِ، فَإِنَّكُمْ لَا تَدْرُونَ لَعَلَّ ذَلِكَ يُعْرَضُ عَلَيْهِ، قَالُوا: فَعَلِّمْنَا قَالَ:

61. ʿAbdullāh [b. Masʿūd] said, "If you send *ṣalāt* upon the Prophet ﷺ, do so correctly, for you do not know, perhaps that is presented to him." It was said to him, "Then teach us." So, he said:

قُولُوا: اللَّهُمَّ اجْعَلْ صَلَاتَكَ وَرَحْمَتَكَ وَبَرَكَاتِكَ عَلَىٰ سَيِّدِ الْمُرْسَلِينَ وَإِمَامِ الْمُتَّقِينَ وَخَاتَمِ النَّبِيِّينَ مُحَمَّدٍ عَبْدِكَ وَرَسُولِكَ إِمَامِ الْخَيْرِ وَقَائِدِ الْخَيْرِ وَرَسُولِ الرَّحْمَةِ، اللَّهُمَّ ابْعَثْهُ مَقَامًا مَحْمُودًا، يَغْبِطُهُ بِهِ الْأَوَّلُونَ وَالْآخِرُونَ، اللَّهُمَّ صَلِّ عَلَىٰ مُحَمَّدٍ وَعَلَىٰ آلِ مُحَمَّدٍ كَمَا صَلَّيْتَ عَلَىٰ إِبْرَاهِيمَ وَعَلَىٰ آلِ إِبْرَاهِيمَ، إِنَّكَ حَمِيدٌ مَجِيدٌ، اللَّهُمَّ بَارِكْ عَلَىٰ مُحَمَّدٍ وَعَلَىٰ آلِ مُحَمَّدٍ كَمَا بَارَكْتَ عَلَىٰ إِبْرَاهِيمَ وَآلِ إِبْرَاهِيمَ إِنَّكَ حَمِيدٌ مَجِيدٌ.

"Say: Allāh, send your *ṣalāt*, mercy, and blessings on the Master of the Messengers, the Leader of the Pious, the Finality of the Prophets, Muḥammad, your slave and messenger, the Leader to Goodness, the

87 Al-Albānī said, "The chain of narration is authentic."

Commander to Goodness, the Messenger of Mercy. Allāh, raise him to a station of praise, where the first and last will envy him. Allāh, send *ṣalāt* upon Muḥammad and upon the family of Muḥammad, just as you sent *ṣalāt* upon Ibrāhīm and upon the family of Ibrāhīm, indeed, you are Praiseworthy and Glorious. Allāh, send blessings upon Muḥammad and upon the family of Muḥammad, just as you sent blessings upon Ibrāhīm and upon the family of Ibrāhīm, indeed, you are Praiseworthy and Glorious *(Allāhumma 'j'al ṣalātaka wa raḥmataka wa barakātaka 'alā sayyidi 'l-mursalīn wa imāmi 'l-muttaqīn wa khātami 'n-nabiyyīn Muḥammadin 'abdika wa rasūlika, imāmi 'l-khayr wa qā'idi 'l-khayr wa rasūli 'r-raḥmah. Allāhumma 'b'ath-hu maqāman maḥmūdan yaghbiṭuhu bihi 'l-awwalūna wa 'l-ākhirūn. Allāhumma ṣalli 'ala Muḥammadin wa 'alā Āli Muḥammad, kamā ṣallayta 'alā Ibrāhīm, wa 'alā Āli Ibrāhīm, innaka Ḥamīdu 'm-Majīd. Allāhumma bārik 'ala Muḥammadin wa 'alā Āli Muḥammad, kamā bārakta 'alā Ibrāhīm, wa Āli Ibrāhīm innaka Ḥamīdu'm-Majīd).*"[88]

---

88 Al-Shaykh Al-Albānī remarked, "This chain of narration is weak, as it contains al-Mas'ūdī who was weak because of his confusion."

[T] This is true, as al-Imām Aḥmad said, "'Āṣim b. 'Alī heard from al-Mas'ūdī after his confusion." (*Sharḥ 'Ilal al-Tirmidhī*, 2/748) However, al-Bayhaqī narrated this same narration in his book *al-Da'awāt al-Kabīr* (177) from al-Mas'ūdī through Ja'far b. 'Awn, who was a Kufan and was himself trustworthy. Al-Imām Aḥmad said, "Whoever narrated from him in al-Baṣrah or al-Kūfah, then his narration is authentic." This was quoted by al-Imām Ibn Rajab in *Sharḥ 'Ilal al-Tirmidhī* (2/748). Further, al-Imām al-Suyūṭī explicitly mentions Ja'far b. 'Awn as one of those who heard from al-Mas'ūdī before his confusion. He mentions this in *Tadrīb al-Rāwī* (2/901). Therefore, the strongest opinion is that this ḥadīth is authentic.

It also has another route via Zayd b. al-Ḥubāb, a trustworthy narrator, from al-Mas'ūdī, collected by al-Shāshī (611). Zayd was another Kufan who report-

٦٢ - حَدَّثَنَا يَحْيَىٰ الْحِمَّانِيُّ، قَالَ: ثنا هُشَيْمٌ، قَالَ: ثنا أَبُو بَلْجٍ، حَدَّثَنِي يُونُسُ مَوْلَىٰ بَنِي هَاشِمٍ، قَالَ: قُلْتُ لِعَبْدِ اللهِ بْنِ عَمْرٍو أَوْ ابْنِ عُمَرَ: كَيْفَ الصَّلَاةُ عَلَىٰ النَّبِيِّ ﷺ؟

62. Yūnus, the ally of the Tribe of Hāshim, said, "I said to ʿAbdullāh b. ʿAmr, 'How does one send *ṣalāt* upon the Prophet ﷺ?'

قَالَ: اللَّهُمَّ اجْعَلْ صَلَوَاتِكَ وَبَرَكَاتِكَ وَرَحْمَتَكَ، عَلَىٰ سَيِّدِ الْمُسْلِمِينَ، وَإِمَامِ الْمُتَّقِينَ، وَخَاتَمِ النَّبِيِّينَ مُحَمَّدٍ عَبْدِكَ وَرَسُولِكَ، إِمَامِ الْخَيْرِ، وَقَائِدِ الْخَيْرِ، اللَّهُمَّ ابْعَثْهُ يَوْمَ الْقِيَامَةِ مَقَامًا مَحْمُودًا يَغْبِطُهُ الْأَوَّلُونَ وَالْآخِرُونَ، وَصَلِّ عَلَىٰ مُحَمَّدٍ وَعَلَىٰ آلِ مُحَمَّدٍ كَمَا صَلَّيْتَ عَلَىٰ إِبْرَاهِيمَ وَعَلَىٰ آلِ إِبْرَاهِيمَ.

He replied: 'Allāh, send your *ṣalāt*, mercy, and blessings on the Master of the Muslims, the Leader of the Pious, the Finality of the Prophets, Muḥammad, your slave and messenger, the Leader to Goodness, the Commander to Goodness. Allāh, raise him on the Day of Resurrection to a station of praise, where the first and last will envy him. May Allāh send *ṣalāt* upon Muḥammad and upon the family of Muḥammad, just as you sent *ṣalāt* upon Ibrāhīm and upon the family of Ibrāhīm *(Allāhumma ʾjʿal ṣalawātaka wa barakātaka wa raḥmataka ʿalā sayyidi ʾl-muslimīn wa imāmi ʾl-muttaqīn wa khātami ʾn-nabiyyīn Muḥammadin ʿabdika wa rasūlika, imāmi ʾl-khayr wa qāʾidi ʾl-khayr. Allāhumma ʾbʿath-hu yawma ʾl-qiyāmati maqāman maḥmūdan yaghbiṭuhu ʾl-awwalūna wa*

---

ed from al-Masʿūdī prior to his departure to Baghdad.

'l-ākhirūn. Wa ṣalla 'ala Muḥammadin wa 'alā Āli Muḥammad, kamā ṣallayta 'alā Ibrāhīm, wa 'alā Āli Ibrāhīm)."[89]

٦٣ – حَدَّثَنَا عَبْدُ اللهِ بْنُ مَسْلَمَةَ، عَنْ مَالِكٍ، عَنْ نُعَيْمِ بْنِ عَبْدِ اللهِ الْمُجْمِرِ، أَنَّ مُحَمَّدَ بْنَ عَبْدِ اللهِ بْنِ زَيْدٍ الْأَنْصَارِيَّ – وَعَبْدُ اللهِ بْنُ زَيْدٍ هُوَ الَّذِي كَانَ رَأَى النِّدَاءَ فِي الصَّلَاةِ – أَخْبَرَهُ عَنْ أَبِي مَسْعُودٍ الْأَنْصَارِيِّ قَالَ: أَتَانَا رَسُولُ اللهِ ﷺ فِي مَجْلِسِ سَعْدِ بْنِ عُبَادَةَ فَقَالَ بَشِيرُ بْنُ سَعْدٍ: أَمَرَنَا اللهُ أَنْ نُصَلِّيَ عَلَيْكَ يَا رَسُولَ اللهِ، فَكَيْفَ نُصَلِّي عَلَيْكَ؟ قَالَ: فَسَكَتَ رَسُولُ اللهِ ﷺ حَتَّىٰ تَمَنَّيْنَا أَنَّهُ لَمْ يَسْأَلْهُ ثُمَّ قَالَ رَسُولُ اللهِ ﷺ:

63. Muḥammad b. 'Abdillāh b. Zayd al-Anṣārī – whose father, 'Abdullāh b. Zayd, saw the dream about the *adhān* for prayer – reported that Abū Mas'ūd al-Anṣārī said, "Allāh's Messenger ﷺ came to us in the gathering of Sa'd b. 'Ubādah. Bashīr b. Sa'd said, 'Allāh has commanded us to send *ṣalāt* upon you, Messenger of Allāh. How can we send *ṣalāt* upon you?' Allāh's Messenger ﷺ remained silent until we wished that he never asked that question, but then said:

«قُولُوا: اللَّهُمَّ صَلِّ عَلَىٰ مُحَمَّدٍ وَعَلَىٰ آلِ مُحَمَّدٍ كَمَا صَلَّيْتَ عَلَىٰ آلِ إِبْرَاهِيمَ وَبَارِكْ عَلَىٰ مُحَمَّدٍ وَعَلَىٰ آلِ مُحَمَّدٍ كَمَا بَارَكْتَ عَلَىٰ آلِ إِبْرَاهِيمَ فِي الْعَالَمِينَ إِنَّكَ حَمِيدٌ مَجِيدٌ وَالسَّلَامُ كَمَا عَلِمْتُمْ».

'Say: Allāh, send *ṣalāt* upon Muḥammad and upon the family of Muḥammad, as you have sent *ṣalāt* upon the family of Ibrāhīm, and send blessings upon Muḥammad and upon the

89 Al-Albānī judged this chain of narration as weak.

family of Muḥammad, as you have sent blessings upon the family of Ibrāhīm in the worlds. Truly, you are Praiseworthy and Glorious *(Allāhumma ṣalli 'ala Muḥammadin wa 'alā Āli Muḥammad, kamā ṣallayta 'alā Āli Ibrāhīm. Wa bārik 'ala Muḥammadin wa 'alā Āli Muḥammad, kamā bārakta 'alā Āli Ibrāhīm fi 'l-'ālamīn, innaka Ḥamīdu 'm-Majīd).*' As for sending salutations: you already know.'"[90]

٦٤ - حَدَّثَنَا مَحْمُودُ بْنُ خِدَاشٍ قَالَ: ثنا جَرِيرٌ، عَنْ مُغِيرَةَ، عَنْ أَبِي مَعْشَرٍ، عَنْ إِبْرَاهِيمَ قَالَ: قَالُوا يَا رَسُولَ اللهِ: قَدْ عَلِمْنَا السَّلَامَ عَلَيْكَ فَكَيْفَ الصَّلَاةُ عَلَيْكَ؟ قَالَ:

64. Ibrāhīm [b. Yazīd al-Nakha'ī] said, "They said, 'Allāh's Messenger, we know how to send salutations upon you, but how can we send *ṣalāt* upon you?' He responded:

«قُولُوا: اللَّهُمَّ صَلِّ عَلَىٰ عَبْدِكَ وَرَسُولِكَ وَأَهْلِ بَيْتِهِ كَمَا صَلَّيْتَ عَلَىٰ آلِ إِبْرَاهِيمَ، إِنَّكَ حَمِيدٌ مَجِيدٌ وَبَارِكْ عَلَيْهِ وَأَهْلِ بَيْتِهِ كَمَا بَارَكْتَ عَلَىٰ إِبْرَاهِيمَ، إِنَّكَ حَمِيدٌ مَجِيدٌ».

'Say: Allāh, send *ṣalāt* upon your slave and messenger, as well as his household, just as you have sent *ṣalāt* upon the family of Ibrāhīm. Truly, you are Praiseworthy and Glorious. And send blessings upon he and his household, as you have sent bless-

90 Al-Albānī said, "The chain of narration is authentic according to the stipulations of Muslim, and Muslim has collected it in his *Ṣaḥīḥ* collection [407]." [T] It was also reported by Aḥmad (22352) via al-Imām Mālik, who reported it in *al-Muwaṭṭá* (505).

ings upon Ibrāhīm. Truly, you are Praiseworthy and Glorious *(Allāhumma ṣalli 'alā 'abdika wa rasūlika wa ahli baytih, kamā ṣallayta 'alā āli Ibrāhīm, innaka ḥamīdu 'm-majīd. Wa bārik 'alayhi wa ahli baytih, kamā bārakta 'alā Ibrāhīm, innaka ḥamīdu 'm-majīd).*'"[91]

٦٥ - حَدَّثَنَا سُلَيْمَانُ بْنُ حَرْبٍ، قَالَ: ثنا السَّرِيُّ بْنُ يَحْيَىٰ قَالَ: سَمِعْتُ الْحَسَنَ قَالَ: لَمَّا نَزَلَتْ: ﴿إِنَّ اللهَ وَمَلَائِكَتَهُ يُصَلُّونَ عَلَى النَّبِيِّ يَا أَيُّهَا الَّذِينَ آمَنُوا صَلُّوا عَلَيْهِ وَسَلِّمُوا تَسْلِيمًا﴾ [الأحزاب: ٥٦] قَالُوا: يَا رَسُولَ اللهِ هَذَا السَّلَامُ قَدْ عَلِمْنَا كَيْفَ هُوَ، فَكَيْفَ تَأْمُرُنَا أَنْ نُصَلِّيَ عَلَيْكَ؟ قَالَ:

65. Al-Ḥasan [al-Baṣrī] said, "When the verse was revealed: **{Surely, Allāh and His angels send *ṣalāt* upon the Prophet. O you who believe, send *ṣalāt* upon him, and send salutations to him in abundance.}** [Qur'ān 33:56] They said, 'Messenger of Allāh, we are aware of how to salute you, but how do you command us to send *ṣalāt* upon you?' He replied:

«تَقُولُونَ: اللَّهُمَّ اجْعَلْ صَلَوَاتِكَ وَبَرَكَاتِكَ عَلَىٰ آلِ مُحَمَّدٍ كَمَا جَعَلْتَهَا عَلَىٰ آلِ إِبْرَاهِيمَ إِنَّكَ حَمِيدٌ مَجِيدٌ».

'Say: Allāh, place your *ṣalāt* and blessings upon the family of Muḥammad, just as you have placed it upon the family of Ibrāhīm. Truly, you are Praiseworthy and Glorious *(Allāhumma 'j'al ṣalawātaka wa barakātaka 'alā āli Muḥammad,*

91 Al-Shaykh al-Albānī said, "The chain of narration is *mursal*, but otherwise authentic."

kamā ja'altahā 'alā āli Ibrāhīm, innaka ḥamīdu 'm-majīd).'"[92]

٦٦ - حَدَّثَنَا إِسْحَاقُ الْفَرْوِيُّ قَالَ: ثنا عَبْدُ اللهِ بْنُ جَعْفَرٍ، عَنِ ابْنِ الْهَادِ، عَنْ عَبْدِ اللهِ بْنِ خَبَّابٍ، عَنْ أَبِي سَعِيدٍ الْخُدْرِيِّ قَالَ: قَالُوا: يَا رَسُولَ اللهِ هَذَا السَّلَامُ عَلَيْكَ قَدْ عَرَفْنَاهُ فَكَيْفَ الصَّلَاةُ؟ قَالَ:

66. Abū Sa'īd al-Khudrī said, "They said, 'Messenger of Allāh, we are aware of how to salute you, but how do we send *ṣalāt* upon you?' He replied:

«تَقُولُونَ اللَّهُمَّ صَلِّ عَلَىٰ مُحَمَّدٍ عَبْدِكَ وَرَسُولِكَ كَمَا صَلَّيْتَ عَلَىٰ آلِ إِبْرَاهِيمَ وَبَارِكْ عَلَىٰ مُحَمَّدٍ وَعَلَىٰ آلِ مُحَمَّدٍ، كَمَا بَارَكْتَ عَلَىٰ إِبْرَاهِيمَ».

'Say: Allāh, send *ṣalāt* upon Muḥammad, your slave and messenger, just as you have sent your *ṣalāt* upon the family of Ibrāhīm, and send blessings upon Muḥammad and upon the family of Muḥammad, just as you have sent blessings upon the family of Ibrāhīm *(Allāhumma ṣalli 'alā Muḥammadin 'abdika wa rasūlika, kamā ṣallayta 'alā āli Ibrāhīm, wa bārik 'alā Muḥammadin wa 'alā āli Muḥammadin, kamā bārakta 'alā Ibrāhīm).'"*[93]

٦٧ - حَدَّثَنَا إِبْرَاهِيمُ بْنُ حَمْزَةَ، قَالَ: ثنا - يَعْنِي: عَبْدَ الْعَزِيزِ بْنَ أَبِي حَازِمٍ

92 Al-Albānī said, "The chain of narration is *mursal*, but otherwise authentic." [T] It was also reported by Ibn Abī Shaybah (8636).
93 Al-Albānī remarked, "It is an authentic ḥadīth," and mentioned that it was also reported by al-Bukhārī (4798).

- وَعَبْدُ الْعَزِيزِ بْنُ مُحَمَّدٍ، عَنْ يَزِيدَ، عَنْ عَبْدِ اللهِ بْنِ خَبَّابٍ، عَنْ أَبِي سَعِيدٍ الْخُدْرِيِّ، قَالَ: قُلْنَا يَا رَسُولَ اللهِ هَذَا السَّلَامُ عَلَيْكَ، فَكَيْفَ الصَّلَاةُ عَلَيْكَ؟ قَالَ:

67. Abū Sa'īd al-Khudrī said, "We said, 'Messenger of Allāh, we are aware of how to salute you, but how do we send *ṣalāt* upon you?' He replied:

«قُولُوا: اللَّهُمَّ صَلِّ عَلَىٰ مُحَمَّدٍ عَبْدِكَ وَرَسُولِكَ كَمَا صَلَّيْتَ عَلَىٰ إِبْرَاهِيمَ وَبَارِكْ عَلَىٰ مُحَمَّدٍ وَآلِ مُحَمَّدٍ كَمَا بَارَكْتَ عَلَىٰ إِبْرَاهِيمَ وَآلِ إِبْرَاهِيمَ».

'Say: Allāh, send *ṣalāt* upon Muḥammad, your slave and messenger, just as you have sent your *ṣalāt* upon Ibrāhīm, and send blessings upon Muḥammad and the family of Muḥammad, just as you have sent blessings upon Ibrāhīm and the family of Ibrāhīm *(Allāhumma ṣalli 'alā Muḥammadin 'abdika wa rasūlika, kamā ṣallayta 'alā Ibrāhīm, wa bārik 'alā Muḥammadin wa āli Muḥammadin, kamā bārakta 'alā Ibrāhīm wa āli Ibrāhīm)*.'"[94]

٦٨ - حَدَّثَنَا عَلِيُّ بْنُ عَبْدِ اللهِ، حَدَّثَنِي مُحَمَّدُ بْنُ بِشْرٍ قَالَ: ثنا مُجَمِّعُ بْنُ يَحْيَىٰ، عَنْ عُثْمَانَ بْنِ مَوْهِبٍ، عَنْ مُوسَىٰ بْنِ طَلْحَةَ - قَالَ الْقَاضِي: أُرَاهُ عَنْ أَبِيهِ، سَقَطَ مِنْ كِتَابِي عَنْ أَبِيهِ - قَالَ: قُلْتُ يَا رَسُولَ اللهِ كَيْفَ الصَّلَاةُ عَلَيْكَ؟ قَالَ:

94 Al-Albānī remarked, "The chain of narration is authentic according to the stipulations of al-Bukhārī," and mentioned that al-Bukhārī reported this same narration with the same chain (6358).

68. Mūsā b. Ṭalḥah reported – al-Qāḍī said: I believe from his father, though that is not present in my notes – that [his father, Ṭalḥah b. 'Ubaydillah, one of the Ten Promised Paradise,] said, "I said, 'Messenger of Allāh, how does one utter *ṣalāt* upon you?' He replied:

«قُلِ: اللَّهُمَّ صَلِّ عَلَىٰ مُحَمَّدٍ كَمَا صَلَّيْتَ عَلَىٰ إِبْرَاهِيمَ إِنَّكَ حَمِيدٌ مَجِيدٌ، وَبَارِكْ عَلَىٰ مُحَمَّدٍ وَعَلَىٰ آلِ مُحَمَّدٍ كَمَا بَارَكْتَ عَلَىٰ إِبْرَاهِيمَ، إِنَّكَ حَمِيدٌ مَجِيدٌ».

'Say: Allāh, send *ṣalāt* upon Muḥammad, just as you have sent your *ṣalāt* upon Ibrāhīm. Truly, you are Praiseworthy and Glorious. And send blessings upon Muḥammad and his family, just as you have sent blessings upon Ibrāhīm. Truly, you are Praiseworthy and Glorious *(Allāhumma ṣalli 'alā Muḥammadin kamā ṣallayta 'alā Ibrāhīm, innaka ḥamīdu 'm-majīd, wa bārik 'alā Muḥammadin wa 'alā ālī Muḥammadin kamā bārakta 'alā Ibrāhīm, innaka ḥamīdu 'm-majīd).*'"[95]

٦٩ – حَدَّثَنَا عَلِيُّ بْنُ عَبْدِ اللهِ، قَالَ: ثنا مَرْوَانُ بْنُ مُعَاوِيَةَ قَالَ: ثنا عُثْمَانُ بْنُ حَكِيمٍ، عَنْ خَالِدِ بْنِ سَلَمَةَ، عَنْ مُوسَىٰ بْنِ طَلْحَةَ، قَالَ: أَخْبَرَنِي زَيْدُ بْنُ خَارِجَةَ – أَخُو بَنِي الْحَارِثِ بْنِ الْخَزْرَجِ – قَالَ: قُلْتُ: يَا رَسُولَ اللهِ قَدْ عَلِمْنَا كَيْفَ نُسَلِّمُ عَلَيْكَ، فَكَيْفَ نُصَلِّي عَلَيْكَ؟ قَالَ:

69. Zayd b. Khārijah, the member of the Tribe of al-Ḥārith b. al-Khazraj, said, "I said, 'Allāh's Messenger, we know how to salute you. However, how do we send *ṣalāt* upon you?' He replied:

---

95 Al-Albānī judged the chain of narration as being authentic.

«صَلُّوا عَلَيَّ وَقُولُوا: اللَّهُمَّ بَارِكْ عَلَىٰ مُحَمَّدٍ وَعَلَىٰ آلِ مُحَمَّدٍ كَمَا بَارَكْتَ عَلَىٰ إِبْرَاهِيمَ وَآلِ إِبْرَاهِيمَ، إِنَّكَ حَمِيدٌ مَجِيدٌ».

'When sending *ṣalāt* upon me, say: Allāh send blessings upon Muḥammad and upon the family of Muḥammad just as you have sent blessings upon Ibrāhīm and the family of Ibrāhīm. Truly, you are Praiseworthy and Glorious *(Allāhumma bārik 'alā Muḥammadin wa 'alā āli Muḥammadin, kamā bārakta 'alā Ibrāhīm wa āli Ibrāhīm innaka ḥamīdu 'm-majīd).*'"[96]

٧٠ - حَدَّثَنَا عَبْدُ اللهِ بْنُ مَسْلَمَةَ، عَنْ مَالِكِ بْنِ أَنَسٍ، عَنْ عَبْدِ اللهِ بْنِ أَبِي بَكْرِ بْنُ مُحَمَّدِ بْنِ عَمْرِو بْنِ حَزْمٍ، عَنْ أَبِيهِ، عَنْ عَمْرِو بْنِ سُلَيْمٍ الزُّرَقِيِّ، قَالَ: أَخْبَرَنِي أَبُو حُمَيْدٍ السَّاعِدِيُّ، أَنَّهُمْ قَالُوا: يَا رَسُولَ اللهِ كَيْفَ نُصَلِّي عَلَيْكَ؟ فَقَالَ رَسُولُ اللهِ ﷺ:

70. Abū Ḥumayd al-Sā'idī reported that [the companions] said, "Allāh's Messenger, how do we send *ṣalāt* upon you?" Allāh's Messenger ﷺ replied:

«قُولُوا: اللَّهُمَّ صَلِّ عَلَىٰ مُحَمَّدٍ وَأَزْوَاجِهِ وَذُرِّيَّتِهِ، كَمَا صَلَّيْتَ عَلَىٰ آلِ إِبْرَاهِيمَ، وَبَارِكْ عَلَىٰ مُحَمَّدٍ وَأَزْوَاجِهِ وَذُرِّيَّتِهِ كَمَا بَارَكْتَ عَلَىٰ آلِ إِبْرَاهِيمَ، إِنَّكَ حَمِيدٌ مَجِيدٌ».

"Say: Allāh, send *ṣalāt* upon Muḥammad, his wives, and his offspring, just as you have sent *ṣalāt* upon the family of

96 Al-Albānī remarked, "The chain of narration is authentic. It was reported by al-Nasā'ī, though in a shorter form."

Ibrāhīm, and send blessings upon Muḥammad, his wives, and his offspring, just as you have sent blessings upon the family of Ibrāhīm. Truly, you are Praiseworthy and Glorious *(Allāhumma ṣalli ʿalā Muḥammadin wa azwājihī wa dhurriyatih, kamā ṣallayta ʿalā āli Ibrāhīm, wa bārik ʿalā Muḥammadin wa azwājihī wa dhurriyatih, kamā bārakta ʿalā āli Ibrāhīm, innaka ḥamīdu ʿm-majīd).*"[97]

٧١ - حَدَّثَنَا سُلَيْمَانُ بْنُ حَرْبٍ، قَالَ: ثنا حَمَّادُ بْنُ زَيْدٍ، عَنْ أَيُّوبَ، عَنْ مُحَمَّدٍ، عَنْ عَبْدِ الرَّحْمَنِ بْنِ بِشْرِ بْنِ مَسْعُودٍ، قَالَ: قِيلَ: يَا رَسُولَ اللهِ، أَمَرْتَنَا أَنْ نُسَلِّمَ عَلَيْكَ وَأَنْ نُصَلِّيَ عَلَيْكَ، وَقَدْ عَلِمْنَا كَيْفَ نُسَلِّمُ عَلَيْكَ، فَكَيْفَ نُصَلِّي؟ قَالَ:

71. ʿAbd al-Raḥmān b. Bishr b. Masʿūd said, "It was once said, ʿAllāh's Messenger, you have commanded us to salute you and to send salutations upon you. We know how to salute you, but how do we send *ṣalāt* upon you?' He replied:

«تَقُولُونَ: اللَّهُمَّ صَلِّ عَلَىٰ آلِ مُحَمَّدٍ، كَمَا صَلَّيْتَ عَلَىٰ آلِ إِبْرَاهِيمَ، وَبَارِكْ عَلَىٰ آلِ مُحَمَّدٍ، كَمَا بَارَكْتَ عَلَىٰ آلِ إِبْرَاهِيمَ».

'You would say: Allāh, send *ṣalāt* upon the family of Muḥammad just as you have sent *ṣalāt* upon the family of Ibrāhīm, and send blessings upon the family of Muḥammad just as you have sent blessings upon the family of Ibrāhīm *(Allāhumma*

97 Al-Albānī said, "It is authentic according to the stipulations of [the Two Shaykhs]." [T] It was also narrated by al-Bukhārī (3369) and Muslim (407).

ṣalli 'alā āli Muḥammadin kamā ṣallayta 'alā āli Ibrāhīm, wa bārik 'alā āli Muḥammadin kamā bārakta 'alā āli Ibrāhīm).'"[98]

٧٢ - حَدَّثَنَا مُسَدَّدٌ قَالَ: ثنا يَزِيدُ بْنُ زُرَيْعٍ قَالَ: ثنا ابْنُ عَوْنٍ، عَنْ مُحَمَّدِ بْنِ سِيرِينَ، عَنْ عَبْدِ الرَّحْمَنِ بْنِ بِشْرِ بْنِ مَسْعُودٍ قَالَ: قَالُوا: يَا رَسُولَ اللهِ، قَدْ عَلِمْنَا كَيْفَ نُسَلِّمُ عَلَيْكَ، فَكَيْفَ الصَّلَاةُ عَلَيْكَ؟ قَالَ:

72. 'Abd al-Raḥmān b. Bishr b. Mas'ūd said, "It was once said, 'Allāh's Messenger, we know how to salute you, but how do we send *ṣalāt* upon you?' He replied:

«قُولُوا: اللَّهُمَّ صَلِّ عَلَىٰ مُحَمَّدٍ، كَمَا صَلَّيْتَ عَلَىٰ آلِ إِبْرَاهِيمَ، اللَّهُمَّ بَارِكْ عَلَىٰ مُحَمَّدٍ، كَمَا بَارَكْتَ عَلَىٰ آلِ إِبْرَاهِيمَ».

'Say: Allāh, send *ṣalāt* upon Muḥammad just as you have sent *ṣalāt* upon the family of Ibrāhīm. Allāh, send blessings upon Muḥammad just as you have sent blessings upon the family of Ibrāhīm *(Allāhumma ṣalli 'alā Muḥammadin kamā ṣallayta 'alā āli Ibrāhīm, Allāhumma bārik 'alā Muḥammadin kamā bārakta 'alā āli Ibrāhīm).'"***[99]

٧٣ - حَدَّثَنَا نَصْرُ بْنُ عَلِيٍّ قَالَ: ثنا عَبْدُ الْأَعْلَىٰ قَالَ: ثنا هِشَامٌ، عَنْ مُحَمَّدٍ عَنْ عَبْدِ الرَّحْمَنِ بْنِ بِشْرِ بْنِ مَسْعُودٍ قَالَ: قُلْنَا - أَوْ قِيلَ - لِلنَّبِيِّ ﷺ:

98 Al-Albānī said, "It is a *mursal* chain of narration, though authentic."
99 Al-Albānī said, "This is also an authentic chain of narration, though *mursal*, as we discussed in the previous narration."

أُمِرْنَا أَنْ نُصَلِّيَ عَلَيْكَ، وَنُسَلِّمَ عَلَيْكَ، فَأَمَّا السَّلَامُ فَقَدْ عَرَفْنَاهُ، وَلَكِنْ كَيْفَ نُصَلِّي عَلَيْكَ؟ قَالَ:

73. ʿAbd al-Raḥmān b. Bishr b. Masʿūd said, "We said (or, it was said) to the Prophet ﷺ, 'We have been commanded to send *ṣalāt* and salutations upon you. As for salutations, we know how, but how do we send *ṣalāt* upon you?' He replied:

«تَقُولُونَ: اللَّهُمَّ صَلِّ عَلَىٰ آلِ مُحَمَّدٍ، كَمَا صَلَّيْتَ عَلَىٰ آلِ إِبْرَاهِيمَ، اللَّهُمَّ بَارِكْ عَلَىٰ مُحَمَّدٍ، كَمَا بَارَكْتَ عَلَىٰ آلِ إِبْرَاهِيمَ».

'You would say: Allāh, send *ṣalāt* upon the family of Muḥammad just as you have sent *ṣalāt* upon the family of Ibrāhīm. Allāh, send blessings upon Muḥammad just as you have sent blessings upon the family of Ibrāhīm *(Allāhumma ṣalli ʿalā Muḥammadin kamā ṣallayta ʿalā āli Ibrāhīm, Allāhumma bārik ʿalā Muḥammadin kamā bārakta ʿalā āli Ibrāhīm).*'"[100]

٧٤ - حَدَّثَنَا سُلَيْمَانُ بْنُ حَرْبٍ قَالَ: ثنا عُمَرُ بْنُ مُسَافِرٍ، حَدَّثَنِي شَيْخٌ مِنْ أَهْلِي قَالَ: سَمِعْتُ سَعِيدَ بْنَ الْمُسَيِّبِ، يَقُولُ: مَا مِنْ دَعْوَةٍ لَا يُصَلَّىٰ عَلَى النَّبِيِّ ﷺ قَبْلَهَا إِلَّا كَانَتْ مُعَلَّقَةً بَيْنَ السَّمَاءِ وَالْأَرْضِ.

74. Saʿīd b. al-Musayyib said, "There is not a supplication where the person does not send *ṣalāt* upon the Prophet ﷺ before it, except that it hangs suspended between the heavens and the earth."[101]

---

100 Al-Albānī remarked, "This chain of narration is authentic, just as the one before it." [T] However, it is still *mursal*.

101 Al-Albānī declared this chain of narration as weak.

٧٥ - حَدَّثَنَا عَبْدُ اللهِ بْنُ عَبْدِ الْوَهَّابِ، قَالَ: ثنا عَبْدُ الوَاحِدِ بْنُ زِيَادٍ، حَدَّثَنِي عُثْمَانُ بْنُ حَكِيمِ بْنِ عَبَّادِ بْنِ حُنَيْفٍ، عَنْ عِكْرِمَةَ، عَنِ ابْنِ عَبَّاسٍ، أَنَّهُ قَالَ: «لا تُصَلُّوا صَلَاةً عَلَىٰ أَحَدٍ إِلَّا عَلَىٰ النَّبِيِّ ﷺ، وَلَكِنْ يُدْعَىٰ لِلْمُسْلِمِينَ وَالْمُسْلِمَاتِ بِالِاسْتِغْفَارِ».

75. Ibn 'Abbās said, "Do not send any *ṣalāt* on anyone but the Prophet ﷺ. However, one may supplicate for the male and female Muslims that Allāh forgives them."[102]

٧٦ - حَدَّثَنَا أَبُو بَكْرِ بْنُ أَبِي شَيْبَةَ قَالَ: ثنا حُسَيْنُ بْنُ عَلِيٍّ، عَنْ جَعْفَرِ بْنِ بُرْقَانَ قَالَ: كَتَبَ عُمَرُ بْنُ عَبْدِ الْعَزِيزِ: أَمَّا بَعْدُ، فَإِنَّ أُنَاسًا مِنَ النَّاسِ قَدِ الْتَمَسُوا الدُّنْيَا بِعَمَلِ الْآخِرَةِ، وَإِنَّ النَّاسَ مِنَ الْقُصَّاصِ قَدْ أَحْدَثُوا فِي الصَّلَاةِ عَلَىٰ خُلَفَائِهِمْ وَأُمَرَائِهِمْ عَدْلَ صَلَاتِهِمْ عَلَىٰ النَّبِيِّ ﷺ، فَإِذَا جَاءَكَ كِتَابِي هَذَا، فَمُرْهُمْ أَنْ تَكُونَ صَلَاتُهُمْ عَلَىٰ النَّبِيِّينَ وَدُعَاؤُهُمْ لِلْمُسْلِمِينَ عَامَّةً، وَيَدَعُوا مَا سِوَىٰ ذَلِكَ»

76. 'Umar b. 'Abd al-'Azīz wrote and said, "As to what follows: Some people have sought the worldly life by way of actions of the hereafter. There are some storytellers who have begun sending *ṣalāt* upon their caliphs and governors just as much as they sent *ṣalāt* upon the Prophet ﷺ. When this letter of mine reaches you, command them to send *ṣalāt* upon the prophets and make supplications for the general body of the Muslims, and then to make other supplications."[103]

102 Al-Abānī said, "The chain of narration is authentic."
103 Al-Albānī said, "It is an authentic chain of narration."

٧٧ - حَدَّثَنَا حَجَّاجٌ قَالَ: ثنا أَبُو عَوَانَةَ، عَنِ الْأَسْوَدِ بْنِ قَيْسٍ، عَنْ نُبَيْحٍ الْعَنَزِيِّ، عَنْ جَابِرِ بْنِ عَبْدِ اللهِ، أَنَّ امْرَأَةً قَالَتْ: يَا رَسُولَ اللهِ، صَلِّ عَلَيَّ وَعَلَىٰ زَوْجِي، فَقَالَ: «**صَلَّىٰ اللهُ عَلَيْكِ وَعَلَىٰ زَوْجِكِ**».

77. Jābir b. 'Abdillāh reported that a woman said, "Allāh's Messenger, send *ṣalāt* upon me and my husband." He replied, **"May Allāh send *ṣalāt* upon you and your husband."**[104]

٧٨ - حَدَّثَنَا سُلَيْمَانُ بْنُ حَرْبٍ قَالَ: ثنا حَمَّادُ بْنُ زَيْدٍ، عَنْ أَيُّوبَ، عَنْ مُحَمَّدٍ، أَنَّهُ كَانَ يَدْعُو لِلصَّغِيرِ وَيَسْتَغْفِرُ كَمَا يَدْعُو لِلْكَبِيرِ، فَقِيلَ لَهُ: إِنَّ هَذَا لَيْسَ لَهُ ذَنْبٌ، فَقَالَ: النَّبِيُّ ﷺ قَدْ غَفَرَ اللهُ لَهُ مَا تَقَدَّمَ مِنْ ذَنْبِهِ وَمَا تَأَخَّرَ، وَقَدْ أُمِرْتُ أَنْ أُصَلِّيَ عَلَيْهِ.

78. Ayyūb [al-Sakhtiyānī] reported, "Muḥammad [b. Sīrīn] used to supplicate and ask forgiveness for the young, just as he would for the old. It was said to him, 'This person has no sins.' He replied, 'The Prophet ﷺ was forgiven for any prior or future sins, but I was also commanded to send *ṣalāt* upon him.'"[105]

٧٩ - حَدَّثَنَا يَعْقُوبُ بْنُ حُمَيْدِ بْنِ كَاسِبٍ، قَالَ: ثنا عَبْدُ اللهِ بْنُ عَبْدِ اللهِ الْأُمَوِيُّ، عَنْ صَالِحِ بْنِ مُحَمَّدِ بْنِ زَائِدَةَ، قَالَ: سَمِعْتُ الْقَاسِمَ بْنَ مُحَمَّدٍ، يَقُولُ: كَانَ يُسْتَحَبُّ لِلرَّجُلِ إِذَا فَرَغَ مِنْ تَلْبِيَتِهِ أَنْ يُصَلِّيَ عَلَىٰ النَّبِيِّ ﷺ.

104 Al-Albānī said, "It has an authentic chain of narration and was reported by Abū Dāwūd (1533).

105 The chain of narration is authentic, according to al-Albānī.

79. Al-Qāsim b. Muḥammad said, "It was recommended for a person, after completing their *talbiyah* (meaning, the invocation to begin the sanctified state of *iḥrām*) that one sends *ṣalāt* upon the Prophet ﷺ."[106]

٨٠ - حَدَّثَنَا يَحْيَىٰ بْنُ عَبْدِ الْحَمِيدِ قَالَ: ثنا سَيْفُ بْنُ عُمَرَ التَّمِيمِيُّ، عَنْ سُلَيْمَانَ الْعَبْسِيِّ، عَنْ عَلِيِّ بْنِ حُسَيْنٍ قَالَ: قَالَ عَلِيُّ بْنُ أَبِي طَالِبٍ رَضِيَ اللهُ عَنْهُ: إِذَا مَرَرْتُمْ بِالْمَسَاجِدِ فَصَلُّوا عَلَىٰ النَّبِيِّ ﷺ.

80. 'Alī b. Abī Ṭālib said, "When you pass by the mosques, send *ṣalāt* upon the Prophet ﷺ."[107]

٨١ - حَدَّثَنَا عَارِمُ بْنُ الْفَضْلِ قَالَ: ثنا عَبْدُ اللهِ بْنُ الْمُبَارَكِ قَالَ: ثنا زَكَرِيَّا، عَنْ الشَّعْبِي، عَنْ وَهْبِ بْنِ الْأَجْدَعِ قَالَ: سَمِعْتُ عُمَرَ بْنَ الْخَطَّابِ، يَقُولُ: إِذَا قَدِمْتُمْ فَطُوفُوا بِالْبَيْتِ سَبْعًا، وَصَلُّوا عِنْدَ الْمَقَامِ رَكْعَتَيْنِ، ثُمَّ ائْتُوا الصَّفَا، فَقُومُوا مِنْ حَيْثُ تَرَوْنَ الْبَيْتَ، فَكَبِّرُوا سَبْعَ تَكْبِيرَاتٍ بَيْنَ كُلِّ تَكْبِيرَتَيْنِ حَمْدٌ لِلَّهِ، وَثَنَاءٌ عَلَيْهِ، وَصَلَاةٌ عَلَىٰ النَّبِيِّ ﷺ، وَمَسْأَلَةٌ لِنَفْسِكَ، وَعَلَىٰ الْمَرْوَةِ مِثْلُ ذَلِكَ.

---

106 The chain of narration is weak, according to al-Albānī.

107 The chain of narration is very weak, as al-Albānī said. However, there is an authentic ḥadīth with the same meaning, from Abū Ḥumayd who reported that the Prophet ﷺ said, "If one of you goes to the mosque, let them send salutations upon the Prophet, and say, 'Allāh, open the doors of your mercy for me,' and when you leave, they should send salutations upon the Prophet and say, 'Allāh, I ask of your bounties.'" It was reported by Abū Dāwūd (465).

81. 'Umar b. al-Khaṭṭāb said, "If you approach [Makkah], perform seven circulations around the House, and pray two units at the standing place [of Ibrāhīm]. Then, approach al-Ṣafā and stand, such that you see the House. Then, utter seven *takbir (Allāhu Akbar)*, and between each two *takbirs* is a praise of Allāh *(al-ḥamdu li 'llāh)*, extolment of Him, and *ṣalāt* upon the Prophet ﷺ. Then, supplicate for yourself. Do the same when you ascend al-Marwah."[108]

٨٢ - حَدَّثَنَا يَحْيَىٰ بْنُ عَبْدِ الْحَمِيدِ قَالَ: ثنا عَبْدُ الْعَزِيزِ بْنُ مُحَمَّدٍ، عَنْ عَبْدِ اللهِ بْنِ الْحَسَنِ، عَنْ أُمِّهِ فَاطِمَةَ بِنْتِ الْحُسَيْنِ، عَنْ فَاطِمَةَ بِنْتِ النَّبِيِّ، ﷺ قَالَتْ: قَالَ لِي رَسُولُ اللهِ ﷺ: «إِذَا دَخَلْتِ الْمَسْجِدَ فَقُولِي: بِسْمِ اللهِ وَالسَّلَامُ عَلَىٰ رَسُولِ اللهِ، اللَّهُمَّ صَلِّ عَلَىٰ مُحَمَّدٍ، وَعَلَىٰ آلِ مُحَمَّدٍ، وَاغْفِرْ لَنَا، وَسَهِّلْ لَنَا أَبْوَابَ رَحْمَتِكَ، فَإِذَا فَرَغْتِ، فَقُولِي مِثْلَ ذَلِكَ، غَيْرَ أَنْ تَقُولِي: وَسَهِّلْ لَنَا أَبْوَابَ فَضْلِكَ».

82. Fāṭimah, daughter of the Prophet ﷺ said, "Allāh's Messenger ﷺ said to me, **'When you enter the mosque, say: In the Name of Allāh, and salutations upon Allāh's Messenger. Allāh, send *ṣalāt* upon Muḥammad and upon the family of Muḥammad. Forgive us and facilitate for us the doors of Your Mercy *(Bis-mi 'llāh wa 's-salāmu 'alā rasūli 'llāh. Allāhumma ṣalli 'alā Muḥammadin wa 'alā āli Muḥammad, wa 'ghfir lanā wa sahhil lanā abwāba raḥmatik)*. After you leave, say the same, but at the end say, 'And facilitate for us the doors of Your**

108 The chain of narration is authentic, as al-Albānī mentioned. Ibn al-Qayy-im also mentioned it in *Jalā' al-Afhām* (263).

Bounties *(wa sahhil lanā abwāba faḍlik)*.'"[109]

٨٣ - حَدَّثَنَا يَحْيَىٰ قَالَ: ثنا قَيْسٌ، عَنْ عَبْدِ اللهِ بْنِ الْحَسَنِ، عَنْ أُمِّهِ فَاطِمَةَ ابْنَةِ الْحُسَيْنِ، عَنْ فَاطِمَةَ بِنْتِ النَّبِيِّ ﷺ قَالَتْ قَالَ لِي رَسُولُ اللهِ ﷺ: «يَا بُنَيَّةُ إِذَا دَخَلْتِ الْمَسْجِدَ فَقُولِي: بِسْمِ اللهِ وَالسَّلَامُ عَلَىٰ رَسُولِ اللهِ، اللَّهُمَّ صَلِّ عَلَىٰ مُحَمَّدٍ، وَعَلَىٰ آلِ مُحَمَّدٍ، اللَّهُمَّ اغْفِرْ لَنَا وَارْحَمْنَا وَافْتَحْ لَنَا أَبْوَابَ رَحْمَتِكَ».

83. Fāṭimah, the daughter of the Prophet ﷺ said, "Allāh's Messenger ﷺ said to me, **'Daughter, when you enter the mosque, say: In the Name of Allāh, and salutations upon Allāh's Messenger. Allāh, send *ṣalāt* upon Muḥammad and upon the family of Muḥammad. Allāh, forgive us and show mercy to us, and open for us the doors to Your Mercy *(Bismi 'llāh wa 's-salāmu 'alā rasūli'llāh. Allāhumma ṣalli 'alā Muḥammadin wa 'alā āli Muḥammad. Allāhumma 'ghfir lanā wa 'r-ḥamnā wa 'ftaḥ lanā abwāba raḥmatik)*.'"**[110]

٨٤ - حَدَّثَنَا يَحْيَىٰ بْنُ عَبْدِ الْحَمِيدِ قَالَ: ثنا شَرِيكٌ، عَنْ لَيْثٍ، عَنْ عَبْدِ اللهِ بْنِ الْحَسَنِ، عَنْ أُمِّهِ فَاطِمَةَ بِنْتِ الْحُسَيْنِ، عَنْ فَاطِمَةَ بِنْتِ النَّبِيِّ ﷺ، عَنِ النَّبِيِّ ﷺ مِثْلَ ذَلِكَ.

84. We have reported the previous ḥadīth through another chain of

---

109 Al-Albānī stated that this is an authentic ḥadīth. [T] It was also reported by al-Ḥākim al-Naysābūrī in *Faḍā'il Fāṭimah al-Zahrā'* (210).
110 The chain of narration is weak, according to Shaykh al-Albānī.

narration as well.[111]

٨٥ - حَدَّثَنَا سُلَيْمَانُ بْنُ حَرْبٍ قَالَ: ثنا شُعْبَةُ، عَنْ أَبِي إِسْحَاقَ قَالَ: سَمِعْتُ سَعِيدَ بْنَ ذِي حُدَّانَ قَالَ: قُلْتُ لِعَلْقَمَةَ مَا أَقُولُ إِذَا دَخَلْتُ الْمَسْجِدَ؟ قَالَ: تَقُولُ: صَلَّىٰ اللهُ وَمَلَائِكَتُهُ عَلَىٰ مُحَمَّدٍ، السَّلَامُ عَلَيْكَ أَيُّهَا النَّبِيُّ وَرَحْمَةُ اللهِ وَبَرَكَاتُهُ.

85. Sa'īd b. Dhī Ḥuddān said, "I said to 'Alqamah, 'What should I say when entering the mosque?' He replied, 'You should say, 'May Allāh and His angels send *ṣalāt* upon Muḥammad. Peace be upon you, O Prophet, as well as the mercy and blessings of Allāh *(Ṣallā 'llahu wa malā'ikatuhu 'alā Muḥammad, as-salāmu 'alayka ayyuha 'n-nabiyyu wa raḥmatu 'llāhi wa barakātuhu)*.'"'[112]

٨٦ - حَدَّثَنَا عَارِمُ بْنُ الْفَضْلِ قَالَ: ثنا حَمَّادُ بْنُ زَيْدٍ، عَنْ مَنْصُورٍ الْمُعْتَمِرِ، عَنْ سَعِيدِ بْنِ ذِي حُدَّانَ قَالَ: قُلْتُ لِعَلْقَمَةَ: يَا أَبَا شِبْلٍ، مَا أَقُولُ إِذَا دَخَلْتُ الْمَسْجِدَ؟ قَالَ: تَقُولُ: صَلَّىٰ اللهُ وَمَلَائِكَتُهُ عَلَىٰ مُحَمَّدٍ، السَّلَامُ عَلَيْكَ أَيُّهَا النَّبِيُّ وَرَحْمَةُ اللهِ. قُلْتُ مَنْ حَدَّثَكَ؟ أَنْتَ سَمِعْتَهُ؟ قَالَ: لَا، حَدَّثَنِيهُ أَبُو إِسْحَاقَ الْهَمْدَانِيُّ.

111 Al-Albānī said of this other chain of narration, "It is weak; however, it has supporting chains of narration that were reported by al-Tirmidhī [314], Ibn Mājah [771] and Aḥmad [26416], but they report his action, not his words teaching Fāṭimah." [T] Therefore, the narration is authentic.

112 Al-Albānī stated that this chain of narration is weak.

86. [Sa'īd][113] b. Dhī Ḥuddān said, "I said to 'Alqamah, 'Abū Shibl, what should I say when entering the mosque?' He replied, 'You should say: May Allāh and His angels send *ṣalāt* upon Muḥammad. Peace be upon you, O Prophet, as well as the mercy of Allāh *(Ṣallā 'llāhu wa malā'ikatuhu 'alā Muḥammad, as-salāmu 'alayka ayyuhā 'n-nabiyyu wa raḥmatu 'llāh).*' I said to him, 'Who told you? Did you hear this?' He replied, 'No, I was informed of this by Abū Isḥāq al-Hamadānī.'"[114]

٨٧ - حَدَّثَنَا هُدْبَةُ بْنُ خَالِدٍ قَالَ ثنا هَمَّامُ بْنُ يَحْيَىٰ قَالَ: ثنا نَافِعٌ، أَنَّ عُمَرَ، كَانَ يُكَبِّرُ عَلَىٰ الصَّفَا ثَلَاثًا يَقُولُ: لَا إِلَهَ إِلَّا اللهُ وَحْدَهُ لَا شَرِيكَ لَهُ، لَهُ الْمُلْكُ وَلَهُ الْحَمْدُ، وَهُوَ عَلَىٰ كُلِّ شَيْءٍ قَدِيرٌ، ثُمَّ يُصَلِّي عَلَىٰ النَّبِيِّ ﷺ، ثُمَّ يَدْعُو وَيُطِيلُ الْقِيَامَ وَالدُّعَاءَ، ثُمَّ يَفْعَلُ عَلَىٰ الْمَرْوَةِ نَحْوَ ذَلِكَ.

87. Nafi' reports that 'Umar would stand atop al-Ṣafā and utter the *takbīr* thrice, then say, "There is no God but Allāh, alone and without partners. To Him belongs kingship, and to Him belongs praise, and He is capable over all things *(Lā ilāha illa 'llāhu waḥdahū lā sharīka lah, lahu 'l-mulku wa lahu 'l-ḥamdu wa huwa 'alā kulli shay'in qadīr).*" Then, he would send *ṣalāt* upon the Prophet ﷺ and would supplicate, standing for a long time while supplicating. Then, he would do the same atop al-Marwah.[115]

٨٨ - حَدَّثَنَا مُسْلِمُ بْنُ إِبْرَاهِيمَ قَالَ: ثنا هِشَامُ بْنُ أَبِي عَبْدِ اللهِ الدَّسْتُوَائِيُّ

113 Al-Albānī said, "In the original manuscript, it said Yazīd, but this could be a typographical error."

114 Al-Albānī said that this chain of narration is also weak.

115 Al-Albānī said that it has authentic chains of narrations.

قَالَ: ثنا حَمَّادُ بْنُ أَبِي سُلَيْمَانَ، عَنْ إِبْرَاهِيمَ، عَنْ عَلْقَمَةَ، أَنَّ ابْنَ مَسْعُودٍ، وَأَبَا مُوسَىٰ وَحُذَيْفَةَ خَرَجَ عَلَيْهِمُ الْوَلِيدُ بْنُ عُقْبَةَ قَبْلَ الْعِيدِ يَوْمًا فَقَالَ لَهُمْ: إِنَّ هَذَا الْعِيدَ قَدْ دَنَا فَكَيْفَ التَّكْبِيرُ فِيهِ؟

88. Al-Walīd b. ʿUqbah approached Ibn Masʿūd, Abū Mūsā, and Ḥudhayfah once and said, "Eid is approaching. How does one do the *takbīr* during it?"

قَالَ عَبْدُ اللهِ: تَبْدَأُ فَتُكَبِّرُ تَكْبِيرَةً تُفْتَتَحُ بِالصَّلَاةِ، وَتَحْمَدُ رَبَّكَ، وَتُصَلِّي عَلَىٰ النَّبِيِّ مُحَمَّدٍ ﷺ، ثُمَّ تَدْعُو أَوْ تُكَبِّرُ وَتَفْعَلُ مِثْلَ ذَلِكَ، ثُمَّ تُكَبِّرُ وَتَفْعَلُ مِثْلَ ذَلِكَ، ثُمَّ تُكَبِّرُ وَتَفْعَلُ مِثْلَ ذَلِكَ، ثُمَّ تَقْرَأُ ثُمَّ تُكَبِّرُ وَتَرْكَعُ، ثُمَّ تَقُومُ فَتَقْرَأُ وَتَحْمَدُ رَبَّكَ وَتُصَلِّي عَلَىٰ النَّبِيِّ مُحَمَّدٍ ﷺ، ثُمَّ تَدْعُو وَتُكَبِّرُ اللهَ وَتَفْعَلُ مِثْلَ ذَلِكَ، ثُمَّ تُكَبِّرُ وَتَفْعَلُ مِثْلَ ذَلِكَ، ثُمَّ تَرْكَعُ.

ʿAbdullāh [b. Masʿūd] replied, "You begin by offering the *takbīr* to begin the prayer. Afterwards, you praise your Lord and send *ṣalāt* upon the Prophet Muḥammad ﷺ. Then, you supplicate or utter the *takbīr* again, and do the same, then you state the *takbīr* again, and do the same, and then you recite. Then [after recitation], you utter the *takbīr* and go into the bowing posture. The, you stand and read, and praise your Lord and send *ṣalāt* upon the Prophet Muḥammad ﷺ. Then, you utter the *takbīr* and do the same, and then you go into the bowing posture."

فَقَالَ حُذَيْفَةُ وَأَبُو مُوسَىٰ: صَدَقَ أَبُو عَبْدِ الرَّحْمَنِ.

Ḥudhayfah and Abū Mūsā both said, "Abū ʿAbd al-Raḥmān has

told the truth."[116]

٨٩ - حَدَّثَنَا عَلِيُّ بْنُ الْمَدِينِيِّ بِهَذَا الْحَدِيثِ عَنْ خَالِدِ بْنِ الْحَارِثِ، عَنْ هِشَامٍ، فَقَالَ فِيهِ: ثُمَّ تُكَبِّرُ فَتَرْكَعُ، فَقَالَ: حُذَيْفَةُ وَالْأَشْعَرِيُّ: صَدَقَ أَبُو عَبْدِ الرَّحْمَنِ.

89. Hishām added, "Then, you utter *takbīr* and go into the bowing position." Ḥudhayfah and al-Ash'arī said, "Abū 'Abd al-Raḥmān has told the truth."[117]

٩٠ - حَدَّثَنَا سُلَيْمَانُ بْنُ حَرْبٍ قَالَ: ثنا حَمَّادُ بْنُ سَلَمَةَ، عَنْ عَبْدِ اللهِ بْنِ أَبِي بَكْرٍ قَالَ: كُنَّا بِالْخَيْفِ وَمَعَنَا عَبْدُ اللهِ بْنُ أَبِي عُتْبَةَ فَحَمِدَ اللهَ وَأَثْنَىٰ عَلَيْهِ، وَصَلَّىٰ عَلَىٰ النَّبِيِّ ﷺ، وَدَعَا بِدَعَوَاتٍ، ثُمَّ قَامَ فَصَلَّىٰ بِنَا.

90. 'Abdullāh b. Abī Bakr said, "We were in al-Khayf[118] and 'Abdullāh b. Abī 'Utbah was with us. He praised Allāh and extolled Him, and then sent *ṣalāt* upon the Prophet ﷺ. Then, he uttered

116 Al-Albānī said that this chain of narration is *ḥasan*.

[T] This was also reported by al-Bayhaqī (6186), who commented, "This is the statement of 'Abdullāh b. Mas'ūd. We follow him in stopping between the *takbīr* that are uttered to utter the remembrances, as there is nothing contrary that has been reported. However, we disagree with him in the number of *takbīr* and in that we believe the *takbīr* should be prior to the recitation in both units. Our evidence is the ḥadīth of Allāh's Messenger ﷺ, and then the actions of the residents of the Two Sanctuaries, and the actions of the Muslims until this very day."

117 Ibid.

118 Al-Albānī said, "It is an area in Minā near the *Jamarāt*."

some supplications and led us in prayer."[119]

٩١ - حَدَّثَنَا مُحَمَّدُ بْنُ كَثِيرٍ قَالَ: ثنا سُفْيَانُ بْنُ سَعِيدٍ، حَدَّثَنِي أَبُو هَاشِمٍ الْوَاسِطِيُّ، عَنِ الشَّعْبِيِّ قَالَ: أَوَّلُ تَكْبِيرَةٍ مِنَ الصَّلَاةِ عَلَى الْجِنَازَةِ ثَنَاءٌ عَلَى اللهِ عَزَّ وَجَلَّ، وَالثَّانِيَةُ صَلَاةٌ عَلَى النَّبِيِّ ﷺ، وَالثَّالِثَةُ دُعَاءٌ لِلْمَيِّتِ، وَالرَّابِعَةُ السَّلَامُ»

91. Al-Shaʿbī said, "[After] the first *takbīr* in the funeral prayer, one utters praise of Allāh the Exalted. After the second, they send *ṣalāt* upon the Prophet ﷺ. After the third is the supplication for the deceased. After the fourth is the *salām* [to end the prayer]."[120]

٩٢ - حَدَّثَنَا عَبْدُ اللهِ بْنُ مَسْلَمَةَ قَالَ: ثنا نَافِعُ بْنُ عَبْدِ الرَّحْمَنِ بْنِ أَبِي نُعَيْمٍ الْقَارِئُ، عَنْ نَافِعٍ، عَنِ ابْنِ عُمَرَ: أَنَّهُ يُكَبِّرُ عَلَى الْجِنَازَةِ وَيُصَلِّي عَلَى النَّبِيِّ ﷺ ثُمَّ يَقُولُ: اللَّهُمَّ بَارِكْ فِيهِ وَصَلِّ عَلَيْهِ وَاغْفِرْ لَهُ وَأَوْرِدْهُ حَوْضَ نَبِيِّكَ ﷺ.

92. Ibn ʿUmar would utter the *takbīr* upon the funeral, and then would send *ṣalāt* upon the Prophet ﷺ and say, "Allāh, bless him, send *ṣalāt* upon him, forgive him, and allow him to be led to the pool of your Prophet ﷺ."[121]

---

119 Al-Albānī stated that this is an authentic chain of narration.
120 The chain of narration is authentic, according to al-Albānī.
121 Al-Albānī said that the chain of narration is authentic. [T] Note that the supplication of Ibn ʿUmar is for the deceased, not the Prophet ﷺ.

٩٣ - حَدَّثَنَا أَبُو مُصْعَبٍ، عَنْ مَالِكِ بْنِ أَنَسٍ، عَنْ سَعِيدِ بْنِ أَبِي سَعِيدٍ الْمَقْبُرِيِّ، عَنْ أَبِيهِ، عَنْ أَبِي هُرَيْرَةَ، سُئِلَ كَيْفَ نُصَلِّي عَلَىٰ الْجِنَازَةِ؟

93. Abū Hurayrah was asked, "How do we pray over the funeral?"

قَالَ: أَنَا لَعَمْرُ اللهِ أُخْبِرُكَ: أَتْبَعُهَا مِنْ أَهْلِهَا فَإِذَا وُضِعَتْ كَبَّرْتُ وَحَمِدْتُ اللهَ وَصَلَّيْتُ عَلَىٰ نَبِيِّهِ ﷺ ثُمَّ أَقُولُ: اللَّهُمَّ هَذَا عَبْدُكَ ابْنُ عَبْدِكَ وَابْنُ أُمَّتِكَ، كَانَ يَشْهَدُ أَنْ لَا إِلَهَ إِلَّا أَنْتَ وَأَنَّ مُحَمَّدًا عَبْدُكَ وَرَسُولُكَ وَأَنْتَ أَعْلَمُ بِهِ، اللَّهُمَّ إِنْ كَانَ مُحْسِنًا فَزِدْ مِنْ إِحْسَانِهِ، وَإِنْ كَانَ مُسِيئًا فَتَجَاوَزْ عَنْهُ، اللَّهُمَّ لَا تَحْرِمْنَا أَجْرَهُ، وَلَا تَفْتِنَّا بَعْدَهُ.

He replied, "By the Life of Allāh, I shall tell you. I follow the funeral from its family. When it is placed, I state the *takbīr*, praise Allāh, send *ṣalāt* upon the Prophet ﷺ and then say: Allāh, this is Your slave, the child of Your male slave, the child of Your female slave. He testified that there is no God but You, and that Muḥammad is Your slave and messenger, and You know best about him. Allāh, if he had done good, increase him in goodness, and if he committed evil, pardon him. Allāh, do not prevent us from his rewards, and do not test us after him *(Allāhumma hadhā 'abduka wa 'bnu 'abdika wa 'bnu amatik, kāna yashhadu a'llā ilāha illā anta wa anna Muḥammadan 'abduka wa rasūlika, wa anta a'lamu bihi. Allāhumma in kāna muḥsinan fa-zid fī iḥsānih, wa in kāna musī'an fatajāwaz 'anhu. Allāhumma lā taḥrimnā ajrahu wa lā taftinnā ba'dahu)*."[122]

---

122 The chain of narration is authentic, and this was collected by *al-Muwaṭṭā* (775), according to al-Albānī.

٩٤ - حَدَّثَنَا مُحَمَّدُ بْنُ الْمُثَنَّىٰ قَالَ: ثنا عَبْدُ الْأَعْلَىٰ قَالَ: ثنا مَعْمَرٌ، عَنِ الزُّهْرِيِّ قَالَ: سَمِعْتُ أَبَا أُمَامَةَ بْنَ سَهْلِ بْنِ حُنَيْفٍ، يُحَدِّثُ سَعِيدَ بْنَ الْمُسَيِّبِ قَالَ: إِنَّ السُّنَّةَ فِي صَلَاةِ الْجِنَازَةِ أَنْ يَقْرَأَ بِفَاتِحَةِ الْكِتَابِ، وَيُصَلِّيَ عَلَىٰ النَّبِيِّ ﷺ، ثُمَّ يُخْلِصَ الدُّعَاءَ لِلْمَيِّتِ مَتَىٰ يَفْرُغُ، وَلَا يَقْرَأُ إِلَّا مَرَّةً وَاحِدَةً ثُمَّ يُسَلِّمَ فِي نَفْسِهِ.

94. Al-Zuhrī said, "I heard Abū Umāmah b. Sahl b. Ḥunayf tell Saʿīd b. al-Musayyib, "During the funeral prayer, the Sunnah is to recite the Beginning of the Book, send *ṣalāt* upon the Prophet ﷺ, supplicate sincerely for the deceased until it is over. One should not recite [Fātiḥah] more than once [after the first *takbīr*], and then should say the *salām* within themselves."[123]

٩٥ - حَدَّثَنَا نَصْرُ بْنُ عَلِيٍّ قَالَ: ثنا خَالِدُ بْنُ يَزِيدَ، عَنْ أَبِي جَعْفَرٍ، عَنِ الرَّبِيعِ بْنِ أَنَسٍ، عَنْ أَبِي الْعَالِيَةِ، ﴿إِنَّ اللَّهَ وَمَلَائِكَتَهُ يُصَلُّونَ عَلَى النَّبِيِّ﴾ [الأحزاب: ٥٦] ﷺ، قَالَ: صَلَاةُ اللهِ عَزَّ وَجَلَّ عَلَيْهِ ثَنَاؤُهُ عَلَيْهِ، وَصَلَاةُ الْمَلَائِكَةِ عَلَيْهِ الدُّعَاءُ.

95. Abu ʻl-ʻĀliyah, commented on the verse: **{Surely, Allāh and His angels send *ṣalāt* upon the Prophet. O you who believe, send *ṣalāt* upon him, and send salutations to him in abundance.}** [Qurʾān 33:56] He said, "The *ṣalāt* of Allāh the Exalted upon him is His praise of him, and the *ṣalāt* of the angels is supplication."[124]

---

123 Al-Albānī said that this chain of narration is authentic. [T] It was also reported by ʻAbd al-Razzāq (6428) and Ibn Abī Shaybah (11379).

124 Al-Albānī said this chain of narration is of the *ḥasan* grade. [T] It was

٩٦ - حَدَّثَنَا نَصْرُ بْنُ عَلِيٍّ قَالَ: ثنا مُحَمَّدُ بْنُ سَوَاءٍ، عَنْ جُوَيْبِرٍ، عَنِ الضَّحَّاكِ قَالَ: صَلَاةُ اللهِ: رَحْمَتُهُ، وَصَلَاةُ الْمَلَائِكَةِ: الدُّعَاءُ.

96. Al-Ḍaḥḥāk said, "The *ṣalāt* of Allāh the Exalted is His Mercy, and the *ṣalāt* of the angels is supplication."[125]

٩٧ - وَحَدَّثَنَاهُ مُحَمَّدُ بْنُ أَبِي بَكْرٍ، ثنا مُحَمَّدُ بْنُ سَوَاءٍ قَالَ: ثنا جُوَيْبِرٌ، عَنِ الضَّحَّاكِ، ﴿هُوَ الَّذِي يُصَلِّي عَلَيْكُمْ وَمَلَائِكَتُهُ﴾ [الأحزاب: ٤٣] قَالَ: صَلَاةُ اللهِ: مَغْفِرَتُهُ، وَصَلَاةُ الْمَلَائِكَةِ: الدُّعَاءُ.

97. Al-Ḍaḥḥāk commented on the verse: **{It is He who sends *ṣalāt* upon you, as do His angels.}** [Qur'ān 33:43] He said, "The *ṣalāt* of Allāh the Exalted is His forgiveness, and the *ṣalāt* of the angels is supplication."[126]

---

reported by al-Bukhārī under the chapter heading, "Chapter: His Statement **{Surely, Allāh and His angels send *ṣalāt* upon the Prophet. O you who believe, send *ṣalāt* upon him, and send salutations to him in abundance}**," and then quoted Abu 'l-'Āliyah authoritatively, with a wording that indicates that Abu 'l-'Āliyah definitively said the wording, though he omitted the chain of narration. Ibn Ḥajar said, "When he reports a ḥadīth without a chain of narration, but states authoritatively that the person quoted said the narration, it is authentic up until the one being quoted." (*Al-Nukat 'alā Kitāb Ibn al-Ṣalāḥ*, 1/325) Contrary to that is if al-Bukhārī reports it in what is known as *ṣīghat al-tamrīḍ* (such as by saying, "it was said," versus definitively saying, "he said") for if that is the case, it could be authentic, *ḥasan*, or weak. This narration was quoted by al-Bukhārī authoritatively, so it is authentic.

125 Al-Albānī said it has a very weak chain of narration.

126 Like the narration before it, it has a very weak chain of narration, as stated by al-Albānī.

٩٨ - حَدَّثَنَا عَبْدُ اللهِ بْنُ مَسْلَمَةَ، عَنْ مَالِكٍ، عَنْ عَبْدِ اللهِ بْنِ دِينَارٍ، أَنَّهُ قَالَ: رَأَيْتُ عَبْدَ اللهِ بْنَ عُمَرَ يَقِفُ عَلَىٰ قَبْرِ النَّبِيِّ ﷺ وَيُصَلِّي عَلَىٰ النَّبِيِّ ﷺ وَأَبِي بَكْرٍ وَعُمَرَ رَضِيَ اللهُ عَنْهُمَا.

98. ʿAbdullāh b. Dīnār reported, "I saw ʿAbdullāh b. ʿUmar stand at the grave of the Prophet ﷺ and send *ṣalāt* upon the Prophet ﷺ. I also saw Abū Bakr and ʿUmar ﷺ do the same."[127]

٩٩ - حَدَّثَنَا عَلِيٌّ قَالَ: ثنا سُفْيَانُ، حَدَّثَنِي عَبْدُ اللهِ بْنُ دِينَارٍ قَالَ: رَأَيْتُ ابْنَ عُمَرَ إِذَا قَدِمَ مِنَ سَفَرٍ دَخَلَ الْمَسْجِدَ، فَقَالَ: السَّلَامُ عَلَيْكَ يَا رَسُولَ اللهِ، السَّلَامُ عَلَىٰ أَبِي بَكْرٍ، السَّلَامُ عَلَىٰ أَبِي، وَيُصَلِّي رَكْعَتَيْنِ.

99. ʿAbdullāh b. Dīnār said, "I saw Ibn ʿUmar: When he would return from travel, he would enter the mosque and say, 'Peace be upon you, Messenger of Allāh; peace be upon Abū Bakr; peace be upon my father,' and would offer two units of prayer."[128]

١٠٠ - حَدَّثَنَا سُلَيْمَانُ بْنُ حَرْبٍ قَالَ: ثنا حَمَّادُ بْنُ زَيْدٍ، عَنْ أَيُّوبَ، عَنْ نَافِعٍ، أَنَّ ابْنَ عُمَرَ كَانَ إِذَا قَدِمَ مِنْ سَفَرٍ دَخَلَ الْمَسْجِدَ ثُمَّ أَتَىٰ الْقَبْرَ فَقَالَ: السَّلَامُ عَلَيْكَ يَا رَسُولَ اللهِ، السَّلَامُ عَلَيْكَ يَا أَبَا بَكْرٍ، السَّلَامُ عَلَيْكَ يَا أَبَتَاهُ.

100. Nāfiʿ reported, "When Ibn ʿUmar would return from travel, he

---

127 Al-Albānī judged it as authentic. [T] It was also collected in the *Muwaṭṭá* of al-Imām Mālik (458), as per the narration of al-Laythī.

128 Al-Albānī said it has an authentic chain of narration.

would enter the mosque, would approach the grave and say, 'Peace be upon you, Messenger of Allāh; peace be upon you, Abū Bakr; peace be upon you, my father.'"[129]

١٠١ - حَدَّثَنِي إِسْحَاقُ بْنُ مُحَمَّدٍ قَالَ: ثنا عَبْدُ اللهِ بْنُ عُمَرَ، عَنْ نَافِعٍ، أَنَّ ابْنَ عُمَرَ، كَانَ إِذَا قَدِمَ مِنْ سَفَرٍ صَلَّىٰ سَجْدَتَيْنِ فِي الْمَسْجِدِ، ثُمَّ يَأْتِي النَّبِيَّ ﷺ فَيَضَعُ يَدَهُ الْيَمِينَ عَلَىٰ قَبْرِ النَّبِيِّ ﷺ وَيَسْتَدْبِرُ الْقِبْلَةَ ثُمَّ يُسَلِّمُ عَلَىٰ النَّبِيِّ ﷺ، ثُمَّ عَلَىٰ أَبِي بَكْرٍ وَعُمَرَ رَضِيَ اللهُ عَنْهُمَا.

101. Nāfi' reported, "When Ibn 'Umar would return from travel, he would pray two units in the mosque, then would approach the Prophet ﷺ and place his right hand on the grave of the Prophet ﷺ, facing away from the *qiblah*. He would then salute the Prophet ﷺ, Abū Bakr, and 'Umar ﷺ."[130]

١٠٢ - حَدَّثَنَا مُعَاذُ بْنُ أَسَدٍ قَالَ: ثنا عَبْدُ اللهِ بْنُ الْمُبَارَكِ، أَخْبَرَنَا ابْنُ لَهِيعَةَ، حَدَّثَنِي خَالِدُ بْنُ يَزِيدَ، عَنْ سَعِيدِ بْنِ أَبِي هِلَالٍ، عَنْ مُنَبِّهِ بْنِ وَهْبٍ، أَنَّ كَعْبًا دَخَلَ عَلَىٰ عَائِشَةَ فَذَكَرُوا رَسُولَ اللهِ ﷺ.

102. Munabbih b. Wahb reported that Ka'b visited 'Ā'ishah and they spoke of Allāh's Messenger ﷺ.

---

129 Al-Albānī said it has an authentic chain of narration. [T] It was also collected by 'Abd al-Razzāq (6724) and Ibn Abī Shaybah (11793).

130 It has a weak chain of narration, and the wording contradicts the other two authentic narrations above it. The weak portion in particular is where Ibn 'Umar would place his hand upon the grave of the Prophet ﷺ, as stated by al-Albānī.

فَقَالَ كَعْبٌ: مَا مِنْ فَجْرٍ يَطْلُعُ إِلَّا وَيُنَزَّلُ سَبْعُونَ أَلْفًا مِنَ الْمَلَائِكَةِ حَتَّىٰ يَحُفُّوا بِالْقَبْرِ يَضْرِبُونَ بِأَجْنِحَتِهِمْ وَيُصَلُّونَ عَلَىٰ النَّبِيِّ ﷺ حَتَّىٰ إِذَا أَمْسَوْا عَرَجُوا وَهَبَطَ سَبْعُونَ أَلْفًا حَتَّىٰ يَحُفُّوا بِالْقَبْرِ، يَضْرِبُونَ بِأَجْنِحَتِهِمْ فَيُصَلُّونَ عَلَىٰ النَّبِيِّ ﷺ: سَبْعُونَ أَلْفًا بِاللَّيْلِ وَسَبْعُونَ أَلْفًا بِالنَّهَارِ، حَتَّىٰ إِذَا انْشَقَّتِ الْأَرْضُ خَرَجَ فِي سَبْعِينَ أَلْفًا مِنَ الْمَلَائِكَةِ يَزِفُّونَهُ.

Kaʿb said, "Every morning, seventy thousand angels descend and surround the grave. They flutter their wings and send *ṣalāt* upon the Prophet ﷺ. When the night approaches, they ascend, and another seventy thousand descend, surrounding the grave, fluttering their wings, and sending *ṣalāt* upon the Prophet ﷺ. There are seventy thousand at night, and seventy thousand during the day, until when the earth is cleft asunder, he is taken from his grave in the midst of seventy thousand angels who will be rushing around him."[131]

١٠٣ - حَدَّثَنَا عَلِيُّ بْنُ عَبْدِ اللهِ قَالَ: ثنا سُفْيَانُ قَالَ: ثنا ابْنُ أَبِي نَجِيحٍ، عَنْ مُجَاهِدٍ: ﴿وَرَفَعْنَا لَكَ ذِكْرَكَ﴾ [الشرح: ٤] قَالَ: لَا أُذْكَرُ إِلَّا ذُكِرْتَ أَشْهَدُ أَنْ لَا إِلَهَ إِلَّا اللهُ، أَشْهَدُ أَنَّ مُحَمَّدًا رَسُولُ اللهِ.

103. Mujāhid said, when commenting on the verse: **{And We raised high your name.}** [Qur'ān 94:4] He said, "[Meaning:] 'I am not mentioned except that you are mentioned, [as occurs in:] I testify that there is no God but Allāh and that Muḥammad is the Messenger of Allāh.'"[132]

---

131 The chain of narration consists of only trustworthy narrators, according to al-Albānī.

132 The chain of narration is authentic, according to al-Albānī.

١٠٤ - حَدَّثَنَا مُحَمَّدُ بْنُ عُبَيْدٍ قَالَ: ثنا مُحَمَّدُ بْنُ ثَوْرٍ، عَنْ مَعْمَرٍ، عَنْ قَتَادَةَ، ﴿وَرَفَعْنَا لَكَ ذِكْرَكَ﴾ [الشرح: ٤] فَقَالَ النَّبِيُّ ﷺ: «**ابْدَءُوا بِالْعُبُودِيَّةِ وَثَنُّوا بِالرِّسَالَةِ**»، قَالَ مَعْمَرٌ: أَشْهَدُ أَنْ لَا إِلَهَ إِلَّا اللهُ وَأَنَّ مُحَمَّدًا عَبْدُهُ: فَهَذَا الْعُبُودِيَّةُ، وَرَسُولُهُ أَنْ يَقُولَ: عَبْدُهُ وَرَسُولُهُ.

104. Qatādah reported about the verse: **{And We raised high your name.}** [Qur'ān 94:4] The Prophet ﷺ said, **"Start with servitude, then mention the message secondly."** Maʿmar said, "I testify that there is no God but Allāh, and that Muḥammad is His slave (this portion contains the servitude), and His Messenger [which contains the message]. [So therefore you say], 'His slave and Messenger.'"[133]

١٠٥ - حَدَّثَنَا عَمْرُو بْنُ مَرْزُوقٍ، ثنا زُهَيْرٌ، عَنْ أَبِي إِسْحَاقَ، أَنَّهُ رَآهُمْ يَسْتَقْبِلُونَ الْإِمَامَ إِذَا خَطَبَ وَلَكِنَّهُمْ كَانُوا لَا يَسْعَوْنَ إِنَّمَا هُوَ قَصَصٌ وَصَلَاةٌ عَلَى النَّبِيِّ ﷺ.

105. Abū Isḥāq [al-Subayʿī] reported that he saw that they would face the *imām* when he gave the sermon. However, they would not

---

[T] Al-Shaykh al-Albānī remarked here that this is a *mursal* narration because it appears to be a *ḥadīth qudsī*. However, the correct understanding is simply that this is the exegesis of the verse offered by Mujāhid ﷺ. As such, the chain of narration is authentic to Mujāhid, and this is his interpretation. This was also the interpretation offered by al-Ṭabarī in explaining this verse, saying, "[Allāh] is saying: I am not mentioned, except that you are mentioned with Me,' and that occurs in the statement of: 'There is no God but Allāh, and Muḥammad is the Messenger of Allāh.'"

133 Al-Albānī said that the chain of narration is authentic, though *mursal*.

rush; they would hear stories and *ṣalāt* upon the Prophet ﷺ.[134]

١٠٦ - حَدَّثَنَا مُحَمَّدُ بْنُ أَبِي بَكْرٍ قَالَ: ثنا عَبْدُ اللهِ بْنُ يَزِيدَ، حَدَّثَنِي حَيْوَةُ، أَخْبَرَنِي أَبُو هَانِئٍ حُمَيْدُ بْنُ هَانِئٍ، أَنَّ أَبَا عَلِيٍّ عَمْرَو بْنَ مَالِكٍ حَدَّثَهُ، أَنَّهُ سَمِعَ فَضَالَةَ بْنَ عُبَيْدٍ - صَاحِبَ رَسُولِ اللهِ ﷺ - يَقُولُ: سَمِعَ رَسُولُ اللهِ رَجُلًا يَدْعُو فِي صَلَاتِهِ لَمْ يُمَجِّدِ اللهَ وَلَمْ يُصَلِّ عَلَى النَّبِيِّ ﷺ فَقَالَ رَسُولُ اللهِ ﷺ: **«عَجِلَ هَذَا»**، ثُمَّ دَعَاهُ فَقَالَ لَهُ أَوْ لِغَيْرِهِ: **«إِذَا صَلَّى أَحَدُكُمْ فَلْيَبْدَأْ بِتَمْجِيدِ اللهِ وَالثَّنَاءِ عَلَيْهِ ثُمَّ يُصَلِّي عَلَى النَّبِيِّ ﷺ ثُمَّ يَدْعُو بَعْدُ بِمَا شَاءَ»**.

106. Faḍālah b. ʿUbayd, the companion of Allāh's Messenger ﷺ said that Allāh's Messenger ﷺ once heard a man supplicating in his prayer and he did not praise Allāh nor send *ṣalāt* upon the Prophet ﷺ. Allāh's Messenger ﷺ said, **"This man has hastened."** Then, he called him over and said to him, or to someone else, **"When one of you prays, they should begin with praise and extolling of Allāh, then send *ṣalāt* upon the Prophet ﷺ, then supplicate with whatever they wish."**[135]

١٠٧ - حَدَّثَنَا مُحَمَّدُ بْنُ الْمُثَنَّى قَالَ: ثنا مُعَاذُ بْنُ هِشَامٍ: حَدَّثَنِي أَبِي، عَنْ قَتَادَةَ، عَنْ عَبْدِ اللهِ بْنِ الْحَارِثِ، أَنَّ أَبَا حَلِيمَةَ - مُعَاذًا - كَانَ يُصَلِّي عَلَى النَّبِيِّ ﷺ فِي الْقُنُوتِ.

134 Al-Albānī said that this is an authentic chain of narration.

135 Al-Albānī said it has a *ḥasan* chain of narration. [T] It was also reported by Abū Dāwūd (1481), al-Tirmidhī (3784) – who called it of the grade *ḥasan ṣaḥīḥ*, and al-Nasāʾī (1208).

107. 'Abdullāh b. al-Ḥārith reported that Abū Ḥalīmah (Mu'ādh [b. al-Ḥārith al-Anṣārī]) used to send *ṣalāt* upon the Prophet ﷺ during his *qunūt* supplication.[136]

❁❁❁

تم الكتاب

This is the ending of the book.

الحمد لله وحده، وصلواته على سيدنا محمد وآله وسلم.

All praise belongs to Allāh, Alone, and may His *ṣalāt* be sent upon our master, Muḥammad and his family, and may salutations be sent as well.

136 Al-Albānī mentioned that this is an authentic chain of narration.